Daddy Issues

Tammy Campbell Brooks

Daddy Issues

Author: Tammy Campbell Brooks
Title: Daddy Issues
Subject: Adult non-fiction
African American
Publishing 2020
Paradeyez Books
ISBN-13:
978-1-7322768-6-4
Library of Congress Control Number:2020912623

Table of Contents

Contents

Daddy Issues
Dedicated to
my son, Bobby Ray King Jr.
and daughter, Tahirah Jessayln Brooks.

Note From Daughter

Daddy Issues focuses on my mother's past relationships with men. Some of them are romantic and others were relationships with men in her family. She takes you down memory lane to figure out some of the reasons behind the good and bad decisions she made when it came to men. She talks about her dad and how much of an impact he had in raising her, and the effect of how he was taken from her. The loss of her dad along with her identity crisis kept her in constant turmoil.

When you read *Daddy Issues*, you will go through a plethora of different emotions. There are numerous stories that will keep the reader cycling through laughter, happiness, and sadness. In addition, there are a lot of interesting stories that will make you eager to know more and will be quite the page turner!

The message of this book can be easily interpreted: my mom's first love was her father. A father should set an example to his daughters about how a man should treat them and he should offer a sense of security, protection, and most importantly, love.

There are many people with *Daddy Issues*. Some don't realize that they suffer from unresolved emotions stemming from a lack or loss of love from the paternal parent. Many choose not to deal with it and cope the best way they know how.

My mom has put her issues in a book for all to read and understand, and just like in the prequel, *The Ghetto Blues,* she doesn't hold back. Her story continues to be captivating, funny, unforgettable, and inspiring.
I hope you enjoy reading my mother's story as much as I did.

Tahirah J. Brooks

Daddy Issues

Daddy Issues

Books by Tammy Campbell Brooks:

The Ghetto Blues (Prequel)

Tar Baby

Tar Baby 2 "Tianna's Story"

Unapologetic Poetic

Chapter One

Left In The Oven Too Long

It's strange how elementary-age children notice differences in you before you notice them in yourself. Family and friends will see the big pink elephant in the room, but won't tell you that you are about to get hit with the biggest reality check in the blink of an eye.

My identity crisis began at the start of elementary school when my sister Tina, my brother Edward, and I attended Gates Elementary School on the east side of San Antonio, Texas. I was six years old and in the first grade when I proudly introduced my siblings to curious small children. I loved my sister and brother. We grew up in a loving home. There was no difference in the amount of love each of us received. I wanted every kid at school to know *exactly* who my siblings were. I loved going to school with my brother and sister because they could take care and look after me, in case someone tried to bully me. I thought I didn't have to worry about bullying, but what shocked me the most was the biggest bully that I had was my kindergarten teacher.

It was the beginning of the school year in 1974. I had a red, white, and blue book satchel that I kept all my school supplies in. It reminded me of the USA flag. I *loved* my satchel and I was very protective of it. My teacher wanted me to put my satchel in the closet. But I didn't want to. I refused.

"Tammy, put your satchel in the closet with the other children," my teacher demanded.

I sat there and ignored her because I didn't want to take my eyes off my satchel. If I were to put it in the closet with the other children, then someone would steal it. I didn't want to risk it, so I kept my satchel sitting right next to me.

"Tammy, put your satchel in the closet with the other children!"

She appeared to be getting more irritated with me, so I reluctantly obliged. I got up from my table and placed it toward the back of the closet so it would be out of sight in case someone tried to steal it. I went back to sit at my table. The teacher continued talking, but I paid her no mind. All I could think about was my satchel, and what if someone *stole* it? It had my coloring books, crayons, glue, pencils, and my Big Chief notebook inside. I wanted my school supplies. I discreetly got up from my table and walked into the closet to check on my satchel. It was exactly where I left it. I walked back to my table to sit down.

*I just checked on my satchel and it's still in the closet where I left it, but what if someone **steals** it?* My mind continued to ponder.

Oh no, I need my satchel. I've got to go get it!

I got up again and walked to where I put my satchel. I grabbed it by the handle and took it back to my table.

My teacher walked over to me and said, "Tammy, didn't I tell you to put that satchel in the closet?" She was upset. My teacher tried to take my satchel from where it sat beside me, but I grabbed it so she wouldn't take it.

We went back and forth like tug-of-war pulling my satchel, and that's when she lifted her hand and:

SLAP!

My teacher slapped the living daylights out of me.

I cried loud and I couldn't wait to go home to tell my mother, Bobbie Jean, that the teacher slapped me. My mother couldn't believe it when I told her, so the next day she visited the school.

The entrance to Gates Elementary had a lot of steps, and as I was going up the steps alongside my mother I began skipping and taking two steps at a time. I was showing off because Mama was at my school. My mother was ready to go into the office and regulate the teacher who slapped her five-year-old daughter.

I was not allowed to go into the principal's office with her. I had to wait in the front area until she returned. I'm not sure if the teacher was reprimanded or not, but after my mother finished talking to the principal, I was moved to a different classroom. That's where I befriended a white girl named Sally who had two blonde pigtails. She looked just like the little girl Cindy from *The Brady Bunch.*

Shortly after moving into my new classroom, Sally was gone. She left town with her family. I no longer had Sally as a friend, but I had my brother. The more my siblings came around me, the more questions my classmates began to ask.

The questions and stares began in first grade with comments, like, "Ummmm, why don't you look like your sister and brother?" I had no response because I *did* look like my sister and brother. We had the same mother and father. I never said anything to my mother about the kids' questions until I was seven years old, and the teasing and questions continued about my brother and me.

"Oh, what happened to your brother, he was left in the oven too long?" kids said about my brother as they laughed and joked. I thought, all right, that's it. There's definitely *something* different about my brother, sister, and me.

The comment about my brother cut deep. I went to my mother so that I could at least have a response to their questions and stares. I asked her why my skin color was so light and why was Edward left in the oven too long?

Mama kept ignoring my questions until I *finally* got an answer about why my skin complexion was so different.

She told me Terrie and I were left on her doorstep.

Chapter Two

Crabs In a Barrel

𝒢OOOOOO COWBOYS!!! WOOOOO HOOOOOOO"

I sat next to Daddy and cheered as my family watched our favorite team, the Dallas Cowboys.

It was the 1978 Super Bowl. The Dallas Cowboys vs the Denver Broncos in Super Bowl XII.

The confetti flew everywhere on the television, we jumped up and down because Dallas won.

The Cowboys' players were crushing orange crush soda cans. My daddy, Pee Tee, mimicked the same words that the TV announcers, fans, and players said: *CRUSH THE ORANGE CRUSH!*"

It was one of the happiest days in the Campbell household. Our family tradition was watching the Dallas Cowboys play every Sunday. Sometimes I sat on my father's lap while he wiggled his legs, excited and nervous about the game. He wove his fingers together and twirled his thumbs to ease tension.

Daddy was serious about his boys and so was I. I would rarely miss a game with my dad. I knew all the Cowboys' players beginning with the famous quarterback, Roger Staubach. But my favorite player was Drew Pearson. He wore team jersey number 88 and played the wide receiver position. I loved Drew Pearson like I loved my dad and I wanted to marry him. I knew I was too young at the time, but I wanted to grow up to marry the man of my dreams. A little girl's dream. He was good looking and his skin complexion was similar to mine.

I developed a complex because of the teasing at school and began noticing people's complexions. More often than not I looked in the mirror and wondered who I was and where I came from. I mean, I knew I came from my mother, but that wasn't good enough. Something was missing, I just didn't know what.

I looked at a photograph of myself taken when I was about four years old. Mama brought Terrie and me to take pictures at Kmart since we were the only two children not in school. Tina and Edward had a hand-painted photo of themselves given to my mother from her friend Larry.

I noticed there were roaches inside of the picture frame. I tried banging it on the ground to get the roaches out, but they didn't move. I opened the back of the frame, but the more I pulled on my picture, the more it stuck to the glass of the frame until it tore. I kept banging the frame for the roaches to come out, but they wouldn't because they were dead. I got so upset at those roaches that I threw the picture along with the frame in the trash. My mother saw the picture in the trash and took it out. She asked why I threw the picture in the trash and I told her it was because it had roaches and they wouldn't come out. She told me to leave the picture alone and put it back on the coffee table. I did what my mother said, but I watched the roaches and it looked like they were staring back at me. The same stares I got from the kids at school about my brother and my skin complexion. I didn't like it, so when my mother wasn't looking, I took the picture off the coffee table and threw it in the trash. I buried it underneath the other trash so Mama wouldn't see it. I had to get rid of that picture with those roaches.

I saw Terrie's picture, but I didn't throw hers away because it didn't have roaches like mine. I analyzed her photo and noticed that Terrie had a big smile as she held a small red, white, and blue ball. It was similar to the Globetrotters' ball. She didn't look like a little girl. In fact, she looked exactly like my brother. Terrie's complexion was just like Edward's. I continued to ask Mama about my skin color because I no longer bought the story of Terrie and I being left on the doorstep. Terrie looked like my brother, but I didn't. I was being bamboozled by Mama. There was something wrong with me, but I didn't know what.

Maybe Mama should have left me in the oven longer like Tina, Edward, and Terrie. This is what my seven-year-old self-thought.

I wanted to look like my siblings. Instead, I looked like my cousins, Sharon and Tracey.

We looked so much alike that people began calling Sharon and I Big Red and Little Red.
I wasn't "red," my favorite book satchel was red. I didn't look like my satchel! I hated being called Red. I don't know if my cousin liked it either, but she never voiced her disdain.

I stayed with Sharon when I was a little girl. I would go to Lockhart, Texas with my cousins and Aunt Ruth Ann, but they never said anything about my siblings and my skin complexion, and I *know* they saw the difference. I never asked my dad about why I was so different. It must have slipped my mind, but everyone in my family looked alike except me. When Daddy and Mama argued, I thought it was because of me, but it wasn't. It was because Daddy was cheating on Mama with a *white* woman.

I thought back to a time when my mother took me to the doctor's office on Hackberry Street. I always had trouble with my tonsils. We went to the doctor to get medicine and they

11

were going to do a procedure that required me to have anesthesia. Mama explained that they were going to give me medicine to put me to sleep. "Nu unnn, Mama, they can't put me to sleep unless I'm ready to go to sleep," I kept repeating over and over.

"Yes, you are. They're going to give you medicine to put you to sleep." The entire time, I kept telling my mother: "*Watch, they can't put me to sleep.*"

While Mama and I were in the waiting area, I kept looking at a *white* lady pick at her skin. She kept picking over and over at her arms. I asked my mother what was wrong with her and why she kept picking at her skin. Mama whispered to me that she had crabs and was picking at them. *Ewwwwww,* I thought, *she has bugs in her skin?*

I was disgusted with the woman picking her skin and hated that Mama told me why she was doing it.

A short time later, I was called into the back office to get "put to sleep."

"Mama, they can't put me to sleep. Watch." I went on and on. I must have gotten on her last nerve, but she didn't get irritated with me. She had patience.

What seemed like moments later, as we were walking out of the office to get my medicine when the procedure was completed, I whispered to my mother, "See, I told you they couldn't put me to sleep."

My mother started laughing and said, "Girl, you were knocked out." I couldn't believe the medicine put me to sleep. And I kept wondering about the lady that picked her skin because of crabs. I pondered if the *white* lady that Daddy was cheating with had crabs?

One night, my mother, siblings, and I got into our parents' green Oldsmobile. The seats were old and torn and made out of hard plastic. They would pinch and scratch our legs every time we sat on them. In the summertime, they would get hot and burn our legs. We eased onto the seats and took a ride with my mother to go get my dad from that *white* woman's house. She lived in the boondocks. If traveling north, there were no homes on the left side of the street. It was nothing but fields and lots of telephone poles and wires. Mama pulled up to her home and knocked on the front door. The lights were on when we arrived and prior to Mama knocking, but the lights turned off and the dogs began barking as my mother banged on the door for Daddy to come out.

Bam, bam, bam.

"Pee Tee, I know you are in there," is what mama said as she continuously banged on the front door. If Daddy was in there, he never came out. Mama got tired of knocking with no response and got back into the car and we left.

We left Dad there with that *white* woman that had crabs.
I wondered if Daddy had crabs, too.
This was the first time I knew my father cheated, and it was with a *white* woman.

Chapter Three

I Never Looked at Him The Same Again

*T*he brief affair with the white lady didn't last long, and Daddy was back at home like normal, and we were a family again. During this time my brother Edward was having issues in school. It wasn't that he was having trouble, he just didn't like school and wanted to stay home with Terrie and me, but he couldn't. It was the day that my mother took Terrie and I for those Kmart pictures. The picture that I threw in the trash when I was seven years old. We dropped Tina and Edward off at Smith's Elementary school on S. New Braunfels Street that morning. We weren't home long before we received a call from the school stating that my brother jumped out the window because he didn't want to be at school. We drove to Smith's Elementary and my mother went inside. I don't know what happened inside the school. My brother thought he was going home, but no, he had to remain in the class.

Mama didn't play. Edward had to stay at school, and she was taking Terrie and me to take pictures. Our plans were made, and she wanted to get back on task. I felt bad for my brother. He hated school and always cried, and each time he cried, he'd get snot running down his nose. We used to tease him and call him "snotty nose." Even though we teased my brother, we didn't want anyone else teasing him.

14

Growing up as the only boy with three sisters was difficult for Edward. He had to play with us most of the time, or my mother's friends' children, who had daughters, too.

My mother had a close friend named Leverne. She had four children: Evelyn, Erica, Veronica, and Wynette, and they were all similar ages to my siblings and me. We'd visit and stay with them so much that we called them our cousins. Besides, one of my relatives used to date Leverne.

One day, my mother left us at Leverne's home. She lived on Morning View Street on the east side of town. We were in the back room jumping on the bed. We always jumped on the bed when we went to Leverne's house. She would cook us enchiladas, and man, they were delicious. Leverne was a good cook. Anyway, we were jumping on the bed in the back room when I heard my relative come inside the house. Shortly after he arrived, I heard him yelling at Leverne about the house not being clean. We continued jumping on the bed and not really paying him any attention until we heard Leverne crying, telling him, "okay." Laverne and her kids called my relative by a nickname. She cried even louder for him to stop, so we stopped jumping on the bed to see what was wrong with her. Veronica and I walked into the living room to see why Leverne was crying, and that's when we saw my relative holding his belt and whipping her.

When we walked in to see what he was doing, he looked at us through his sunshades. I couldn't see his eyes, but I could see his lips and how they curled. Perspiration ran down his face and found a comfort zone in his mustache. He stopped hitting her with the belt as I looked at him. I was about six years old and I will never forget the day that I saw my relative whipping Leverne with a belt. I never saw an adult get a whipping, and my father never hit my mother or us with a belt.

15

I couldn't understand why he beat Leverne. She was a grown woman, not a kid. And she was a nice sweet lady. She always cooked and took care of us like we were her own children. I didn't tell my relative anything, but I never looked at him the same way after I saw him beating Leverne. It wasn't the first or the last beating that he gave her, according to her children, but it was the first and the last that I witnessed. And I didn't like it.

Leverne's children and my siblings always played together, and there was this white old couple that lived in a duplex house next to where they lived. We would go to their house and get candy. The old man *always* gave us peppermints. He gave *me* something more than candy when we visited him one day. I went to his house to get candy like I normally did, and he asked me to sit on his lap. I jumped on his lap like I did when I sat on my father's lap, and he gave me candy. Once he finished giving me candy, he asked me to give him a kiss. I gave him a kiss and he stuck his nasty tongue inside my mouth. It felt wet, disgusting, and wrong. I ran off after he kissed me in my mouth and I never went back to his house. I never told my parents, but I have no idea why I didn't. I still feel his wet disgusting tongue in my mouth.

He was a child predator.

Chapter Four

Colour My World

We frequented my parental grandmother's side of the family almost weekly. No one in my dad's family treated me differently from my siblings.

Daddy played board games with his mother, sister, and friends all the time. They would drink their beer and play cards and dominoes all night and listen to the Blues.
I'd run in from playing outside and my dad would see me and say, "There goes my 'A' student." I would smile like a Cheshire cat on picture day. I loved it when he called me his "A" student, and he often bragged in front of everyone about my grades. When it was report card time, my dad would say that he didn't have to worry about me because he already knew what my grades were. Instead, he would skip me and go straight to my brother. My dad was the disciplinarian who got on us about our education. He sat my brother down at the table and read his assigned words for him to spell. My brother would get in trouble if he kept spelling the words wrong after Daddy had gone over them a few times. I would snicker and laugh at my brother and my dad would send me to my room. Daddy was tougher on Edward than he was on us girls. The girls rarely if ever got into trouble, but I remember my brother getting into a lot more trouble than us. We were all bad, so I don't know why Daddy was stricter with Edward. He would get after my cousin, Ronnie, for messing with my grandmother Mamie Campbell's wig.

Ronnie had bubbled eyes and looked similar to the actor Chris Tucker. He would run up to my grandmother while she played dominoes and cards, and turn her wig sideways or backward and take off running. He would get her wigs out of her room and put them on top of his head and pretend like he was our grandmother. We would die laughing and no matter how many times my grandmother cursed at him, he still did it. My dad would get after him too, and eventually he would calm down.

Ronnie was my grandmother's favorite grandchild for some unknown reason. His mother, my aunt Debra, would leave him at her house while she worked.

When we visited my grandmother, he was always there and showing his tail in front of us. Ronnie and I were three months apart, but I was older. He wasn't the only one making fun of my grandmother; we all made fun of her when she heard her favorite Blues song play on the record player and she'd had a little too much to drink. She'd yell, "heyyyyy" and hit the table with closed fists, her head bowed, eyes closed, feeling those good ole Blues. Grandma did this a lot. It was her signature move and the one we often imitated.

Whenever my dad visited his mother, he always wanted us with him.

One night, my dad was drunk and wanted to pack us in the car and take us to his mother's house with him. My mother said "no," that he was not taking her kids anywhere because he was too drunk. They argued, but my mom won the argument and we stayed home.

It was good that we stayed home because Daddy got into a one-car accident and wrapped our car around the concrete pillar of the Martin Luther King Drive underpass. He totaled the car and took off running on foot. He had no major injuries, just a few scratches. But if he had taken his kids with him, my mother said that he would have killed us all.

We often went with my father everywhere and that included his job. CrestHaven Nursing Home was making its Grand Opening and my father was the supervisor. We'd go with him to check on the facility to make sure the construction and opening were going as planned before the residents moved in. We enjoyed going with him to hear him play on the black grand piano while we ran around the entire facility just being kids.

While we played hide-n-seek, we could hear my father playing Chicago's "Colour My World." I loved that song and hearing him play it on the piano. It was his favorite and he played it each time we went inside the nursing home. I don't know where he got his musical talent or his love of music, but he instilled it in all of us. When he wasn't playing the piano, he was making us breakfast and being a loving dad.

One morning, when my mother was at work and my father was off, he fixed us cereal while he made himself some eggs. We sat at the kitchen table eating our corn flakes when I smelled something disgusting, almost like poop. I knew Dad was cooking eggs, but it smelled worse than eggs.

Edward said that Daddy farted. As soon as he said it was a fart, I threw up my corn flakes inside into my bowl and my father made me go to my room. My siblings erupted in laughter, but his farts were nothing to laugh about. It almost killed me that morning. Daddy smelled just like the living dead.

Chapter Five

Love Will Keep Us Together

*I*n 1977, *The Captain and Tennille* TV show was very popular. It was a weekly show hosted by a husband and wife. I looked at the married couple and admired how in love they were and how they interacted on television. They were the only happily married couple that I knew on TV or in real life. Except for my aunt Ruth Ann and her husband Big James. I'd never seen my uncle disrespect my aunt and they had been together for years. I remember I used to be so afraid of my uncle, but according to my sister Terrie and my brother, Big James wasn't mean. We called him Big James because my cousin was named after him, and we called him Little James. Growing up, my aunt and uncle had the only loving relationship that I could remember.

One night, we were watching the show when we received a phone call that my father was at the hospital having surgery on his hand. He was working at Dillard's department store at Windsor Park Mall when he stuck his hand between the elevator doors to keep them from closing when someone wanted to get on. Instead of the elevator door opening, it didn't sense my dad's hand and continued to close, smashing his hand between the doors. He was immediately taken to the hospital.

A little before my dad's accident at work, Terrie and I were in our room together and she was messing with the hot iron for some odd reason. I warned her to leave the iron alone, but she kept insisting that it wasn't hot. Before I could stop her, she placed the iron on her face to see if it was hot. It was, and she burned her face. We wondered why Terrie tested it on her face rather than any other place on her body, but she had no answer because she was only around five years old. Thankfully, her face healed and didn't leave any permanent scarring, but my father's injuries were more serious. The accident left a horrible scar. His hand looked like Freddy Krueger's from *A Nightmare On Elm Street*.

Prior to this incident, my dad made decent money working at Dillard's. That was how we got our wooden dinette set and our beloved microwave we later had to sell to move back to Sutton Homes. Sutton Homes was the ghetto. We were in awe of the microwave in the 1970s.

My parents traveled to Lockhart, Texas where my mother and her family are from and would bring home Lockhart sausages, which we would cook in the microwave. They traveled to Lockhart when they got paid. This was during the time they both were working at CrestHaven Nursing Home and before the fight with my father's mistress Rose that cost my mother her job and marriage.

It was during this time that our dog Bobbie, a gray poodle, got sick. Bobbie was named after my mother and he was bad. When we would go on outings, we would leave him home alone and close the door to our bedroom so that he wouldn't get out.

One day, we left the bedroom window open because we had burglar bars. He clawed his way through the window screen so that he could get outside. We came back home, didn't see him, and noticed a hole in the screen. We looked out back and he was in the yard. Bobbie was bad but we loved him like a member of the Campbell family. Years later, he died of mange and my father buried him in the backyard. We cried as my dad put him in his grave.

My father did a lot of things with us growing up. He was a hands-on father. When he wasn't at work, he would do odd jobs around the house like building things. He worked on our cars and he was a pretty good jack of all trades.

I remember after my parent's separation in 1978, when we moved to Sutton Homes, he would meet us at Walters and PanAm Street to spend time with us. We used to meet him at the little red icehouse. The little red icehouse was where McDonald's is currently located. He never came to our house to pick us up because he never wanted to see my mother's new boyfriend, Alfred. My mother wanted nothing to do with my father because of his cheating ways. She had put a lot of her faith in my dad and he broke her trust and spirit. My dad and her kids were my mother's life. She believed in family and did everything in her power to keep the marriage together, but my father still left after thirteen years. He never ever neglected his children, though. He was always in our lives despite their irreconcilable differences. He was not a deadbeat.

My father put his children before the other women he was dating, and despite them having their own kids, no other children came before us. And that included me.

After my mom and dad's separation, she finally confessed why my skin color was so different by telling me that my father, Pee Tee, was not my real dad. He still didn't treat me differently. He would let his friends know that I was *his* daughter as well and not to question anything about me.

One day we were at Rose's, my father's mistress's house, when a guy that my father knew asked about me. My dad told him that we were his kids. "The light-skinned one, too?" the guy asked. "Yeah, her too," my dad responded, cutting him short. My sister and brother were the same way when our friends asked why I was so light skinned. My siblings always said, "She looks like our mother." The kids at school always saw my father instead of my mother, so that was the explanation my siblings used to keep kids from questioning my identity. I knew having to answer questions about me got on their nerves, but they never said anything. They protected and defended the family secret that I had a different father. I was their sister and that's all anyone needed to know.

The constant stares and questions took their toll on me at a young age. I was a happy child until my mother dropped the devastating bombshell about my real father when I was eight years old. That changed how I saw me. I didn't hate myself, I just wanted to be unnoticed, and it seemed like the more I tried to fly under the radar, the more I was thrown into the forefront. I stuck out like a sore thumb, like the sun on a rainy day, or a pig with lipstick. I was a shy little girl and I wanted my mother for protection. She was my place of solace and *my* comfort zone. A place of love and endearment. I gave her no personal space, and wherever she'd go, I was right by her side. Except one day when my mother needed her "me" time and she left us with my aunt.

Mama wanted to go out to the nightclub to relieve her heartache about my father cheating and leaving her for another woman, so she dropped my siblings and I off at my aunt Ruth Ann's house. I didn't want to stay because I was afraid of Big James. I held her tight because it was the first time that I'd ever known her to leave and go somewhere other than work without me. I cried for her as I saw her walk out of my aunt's front door. I wanted my mother! She needed her space to clear her head, but I needed her too. I needed her like the day we pulled into the self-serve station to get gas for the car. My siblings and I were in the back seat when my mother got out of the car to pump the gas. I don't know what she was doing but the gun she carried in her purse fired and she accidentally shot herself in the leg. We were going to visit my grandparents who lived a block from the gas station. She was transported to the hospital and we stayed with my grandparents until she was released. She recovered from her injuries within weeks. I missed her and cried for her return. I didn't want to stay with my grandparents and certainly not when Bennie was there visiting.

My grandfather's relative Bennie was living with them on the day my mother accidentally shot herself. Bennie always cut himself shaving and would scare us to death with toilet paper plastered all over his face to stop the bleeding.

Years later, Bennie was killed riding his bike home from work. He was hit by a car. It was a hit and run. My mother thought he was murdered for insurance money reasons, but it was a rumor and there wasn't any proof.

Mama got out of the hospital and came to get us. We were happy to leave, especially with Bennie looking so scary. He reminded me of the many ghost stories Mama told about her family living in Lockhart. My mom was a storyteller. She talked to me like I was a grown woman when I was a child. She told me stories of her grandmother on her father and mother's sides of the family.

She talked a lot about ghost stories in Lockhart, Texas. She said that she always saw ghosts and that her grandmother, Sammie, was voodooed because she had an affair with another woman's husband. My mom was eight years old when she saw her grandmother being taken to the hospital for hemorrhaging. There were snakes coming out of her when she used the restroom. She never saw her grandmother again after they took her because she had passed away. She was very close to her grandmother and used to help her around the house. My mother claimed that the wife of the man her grandmother was having an affair with had cast a spell on her. A lot of Lockhart folks believed in voodoo. My mother was one of them.

There were stories of tragedies she told, such as her relatives' children dying in a house fire. One of the children had the same name as me. The child was really intelligent and tried to save her siblings but wasn't able to. Her relative never got over the death of her children and she blamed herself for years. My mother always told me tales of her life. I enjoyed each one and could hardly wait for the next story.

Chapter Six

The Other Half of Me

$\mathcal{7}$ enjoyed all my mother's stories until she told me the tale of my biological father, DeWhight Wilson. After she and my father separated, she was ready to come clean as to why my skin color was lighter than my siblings.

She told me how she was working at the Pig Stand on Broadway Street in San Antonio, Texas when she met him. He was in the United States Army. She was twenty-two years old with two children and he was twenty-two years old.

It was 1968 and my dad, Pee Tee, would get drunk and wouldn't pick her up from work. She had to walk home in the dark or wait to see if he showed. So, one day, she met DeWhight and they began to converse.

DeWhight was good-looking and had beautiful teeth. He was classified as an E-3 ranking in the Army. He was born in Denver, Colorado and was stationed at Fort Sam Houston Army Base. He had sandy red hair with a light complexion. She said the only way you could tell he was "Black" was because of his kinky hair.

She and DeWhight became friends and he gave her rides home when my dad was a no-show. He was a good listener and what she loved most about him was that he didn't drink. His behavior was the total opposite of my dad's.

My mother was vulnerable during this time. Daddy was cheating and drinking, and she was young and left taking care of two kids. DeWhight came along and made her feel like a natural woman. Their talks became more and more serious, and she really began to fall for him. My dad going outside of the marriage doing God-knows-what didn't help the situation. My mother decided that two could play the cheating game, and she and DeWhight had sex in the back of his car. They only did it *once*.

During this time, my mother brought DeWhight to her home where she and my father resided. My aunt Dorothy Nell was a teenager. She came to visit and asked my mother, "Bobbie Jean, what is that *white* man doing over here?" My mother explained to my aunt that he wasn't white. He just looked white, but he was Black. Everything about him was Black because he grew up in the ghetto of Kansas City Missouri.

Shortly after the one-night affair with DeWhight, Mama realized she was pregnant with me. She didn't know who the father was until I came out lighter than the baby blanket she carried me in. She was so shocked and dismayed, she was going to abandon me in the hospital, but her mother made her take me home. When my father saw me, he knew I wasn't his daughter, but he didn't care. He told my mother that he loved me just like his own children. My mother, knowing that I was DeWhight's daughter, sent a message to him through a mutual female friend of theirs, but she heard back that he had *allegedly* been stationed overseas. My mom never believed he left. She knew he was still in San Antonio, but he didn't want anything to do with her or me. He preyed upon her vulnerability. He knew she was having trouble in her marriage, so he befriended her, got what he wanted, and left. She never bad-mouthed DeWhight. I felt that she was hoping he'd take her away from her situation with my dad, but when it didn't happen, it was another blow to her self-esteem. She had three children by the age of twenty-three.

I don't know how long my mother and DeWhight courted because every time my mother tried to tell me about him, I wasn't interested. I didn't know DeWhight. I didn't want to know him, and I didn't care to know him. As a matter of fact, I *hated* him for many years. I hated everything about him. The only father I knew and loved was the man that raised me.

Mama never heard from or saw DeWhight after I was born in 1969. She often studied me and said how much I looked like *him*. I had his smile, nose, eyebrows, and his complexion. She talked about a sandy red patch of hair that I had on the top left side of the crown of my head. When she combed my hair, she would make reference to it. I hated that I looked like *him*. An unknown person that I would probably never meet in my life. It gave me an identity crisis. Daddy issues. But my father, Pee Tee, took on the responsibilities of raising me as his own. I became Tammy Campbell from that day forward. He claimed me and gave me an identity. He gave me unconditional love.

Chapter Seven

Tomboy

I did everything my brother and his friends did. When my brother rapped, I rapped. When he pop locked, I pop locked. It was 1978 when we first heard the song "Rapper's Delight." It played on every radio station, but we also had the album. Grandmaster Flash was the pioneer of hip hop. My brother became Chilli J. The "J" was the initial of his first name, James. Everybody in the hood lost their minds when hip hop made its grand entrance. "Rapper's Delight" was so popular that it played on every radio station and every record player in the hood. My brother and his friends rapped and danced to hip hop. I wanted to dance and rap too, so I sometimes hung out with my brother and his friends. I was always doing things that boys did. I saw my brother as my protector since my father was no longer in the home.

One day I was walking to Young's Grocery Store in the Sutton Homes to buy candy. A boy my age named Maurice saw me and tried to talk to me. It was the summer I was going into the sixth grade. He began flirting with me and I ignored him like I did every annoying little boy. He was upset because I wasn't paying him any attention, so he walked up to me and grabbed my behind. I was livid! I folded my tongue behind my teeth and took off one of my sandals, chasing after him so I could hit him with it. He was laughing and running in between the cars, dodging me and my shoe. I threw my sandal at him, but missed. That really angered me. He continued to laugh, which made it worse. I was hotter than fish grease. I wanted to punch him so bad. Since I couldn't catch him, I retrieved my shoe and took off running home to tell my brother that Maurice touched my booty. I was appalled and hurt. I didn't want anyone touching or invading my body. My brother adored me, so when he heard that Maurice touched my butt, he was ready to put a foot in his ass.

My brother and his best friend Pop went to Young's Grocery Store looking for Maurice, but they never found him. Maurice told everyone about the incident and how I cried when he grabbed me. He had eczema that made him look horrible, so of course I didn't want him touching me. I didn't know if he was contagious or not. All I knew was that he was ugly. He also had a twin sister and we sold candy together.

Years later in 1989, Maurice got addicted to crack cocaine and was gunned down in the Wheatley Courts for trying to rob a drug dealer. According to witnesses, he was reaching inside someone's car when he was shot multiple times. It was tragic because he was only nineteen years old, but based on his behavior as a kid, his early death was not a shock. Maurice was only one boy of many that liked me, but I had no interest in any of them. I wanted to do my classwork and walk home without anyone messing with me. But unfortunately, when you live in the ghetto, if you don't start trouble it will inevitably find you. And so will those bad boys.

When boys like you, they often tease you. Pop always teased me and laughed when I turned bright red. He thought me blushing was cute. But to me, he was annoying. We were in the same class in our fourth and fifth grade years. Since Pop was my brother's friend, we always interacted with each other, not only at school, but in the neighborhood too. He lived across the street from me and played with my brother every day.

During Christmas when we were in the fifth grade, we had a party, and my teacher Mrs. Hastings recommended each of us bring an inexpensive Christmas gift to exchange. Each student was supposed to have *one* gift. We all exchanged gifts and I was up talking to friends and playing games. When I returned to my desk I noticed that another gift was on top of it. It had my name on it, but it didn't say whom it was from. I kept asking all the kids, "Who gave me the gift?" No one knew and no one answered. I was baffled. I opened the nicely-wrapped gift and it was a Chinese checkers game. I continued asking who gave me the gift but still no one answered or knew. After the party ended and class was over, Pop came to me and told me that he gave me the gift. I was so upset with him. I knew he liked me, but I didn't want anyone else to know. He was my brother's friend. I hated all boys except for my classmate Michael. I had a huge crush on him because he was smart, and I liked intelligent boys. I felt bad for being so upset at Pop for giving me the gift, but I didn't want anyone to know that he liked me. I was shy and wanted my brother's friends to be my friends, not for them to have any type of affection for me. I considered myself one of them. I was a tomboy.

Pop would get so sad as the summer months approached because he knew that my aunt would be coming to pick me up to live with them until school began. I loved to stay with my aunt during the summer, but the times I didn't stay with her, I would isolate myself in my room and play with my little white baby dolls. I'd play school with them and pretend like I was their teacher. I was very particular about them and would make sure they were well dressed and that their hair was combed. I'd read all kinds of books to them. The books were ones from Columbia House that my mother ordered through the mail. They always had order slips inside the magazines to order books. She never paid a penny for them, and after so many fake names on the forms, they stopped sending us books. Every chance my mother got, she always filled out and sent in forms from different companies such as Fingerhut to order me books.

My favorite childhood book was *Whistle, Mary, Whistle* by Bill Martin. Whenever our fourth-grade class went to the library, I'd put on the audio and follow along with the book. *Whistle, Mary, Whistle* was about a little girl that was offered all types of gifts like pies, jewelry, and animals from her mother if she would whistle. Mary wouldn't whistle until her mother offered her the gift of a man! And that's when Mary couldn't stop whistling. I loved the fact that Mary turned down all the gifts with the exception of a *man*. I had no idea why I was so flattered by this book at such a young age. I loved to read.

When I wasn't playing house or reading to my dolls, I sometimes hung out at the Sutton Homes gym. I'd go play games or basketball, which I was terrible at, but didn't care to master the sport. One sport I did master was wrestling. I would go to the gym to wrestle girls, all sizes, and I was good at it. No one could beat me at wrestling. I had a unique technique that I would always use to get them to the floor. The girls had to think on their toes to counter the move, but I'd make sure they were on the floor first. I was slick with it and no one could counter or defend my strategy. There was one girl named Nicki who always gave me a challenge, but in the end she could never dethrone me. The wrestling move I learned at a young age taught me how to defend myself growing up. Because if you know anything about the ghetto, people were always going to try you. Meaning see how weak you were.

When I was in seventh grade, I had a classmate named Nathanial. His nickname was Quartermule. He was a midget compared to other boys, and some girls too.

One day I was walking down the hallway with my friends going to class, and Nathanial kept throwing balled up paper at my back. I'd turn around to see who kept throwing the paper at me and he was walking with his friends pretending like it wasn't him. I told the boys to throw another paper at me. I dared them to do it again and to see what would happen to them. Nathanial threw the paper and they all started laughing. I stopped dead in my tracks, turned around toward the boys, and that's when my tongue instantly folded underneath my teeth. A signature movement that warns everyone that I'm super mad. I turned to grab Nathanial, but he took off running to a classroom at the end of the hallway near the stairs. I went inside the classroom and pulled him out so that I could beat his butt. I did my tomboy wrestling move once I got him in the hall. I wrestled him to the floor. I don't remember beating him, but I choked him and tried to throw him down the flight of stairs. The teacher in the classroom Nathanial ran inside saw what was going on, so she stopped the fight and we were taken to the principal's office. The principal wasn't in, so we saw the assistant principal, who was a dark-skinned Black man, balding in the center of his head. He wore glasses. He asked Nathanial what he was doing fighting a *girl*. And he told him, "I heard that you got beat up, too," while laughing. Nathanial denied it as he slumped down in his chair with one leg out and the other folded inward like he was so cool. The assistant principal told me to go back to class because he knew that I was a good student and he had never seen me in his office. Nathanial was a bully from a dysfunctional home and he was always getting into trouble. He was suspended, but I wasn't. This infuriated Nathanial and he made threats that he would get me at the end of the school year. My brother attended Emerson Middle School with me, and he was aware of the fight and threats. He wasn't going to let nobody harm me.

On the last day of school, my mother came to pick up my brother and me from Emerson because there were rumors of Nathaniel, his brother Clarence, and their posse coming to get me. But my mom was there waiting on us both along with her best friend, Smith & Wesson. My protector never failed me. If anyone knew my mother, they knew she was *crazy* about her children. You didn't mess with Bobbie Jean's kids. My mother had no rationale when it came to her children. She would shoot first and ask questions later.

Neither Nathaniel, his brother, or their *posse* ever showed up, and to be honest, I'm glad that they didn't because it would have been the *first* ghetto school shooting in history.

Living in the ghetto among poverty and troublemakers was rough, and there was always someone trying you. We had to adapt quickly or get swallowed alive. We were the Campbells and were never about that life, but we never backed down. If you brought shit to us, then we would finish it. We feared no one, not even death. We were willing to die to protect each other.

Chapter Eight

Granddaddy

*M*y mother was the third from the oldest of five children. My grandmother had my mother at the age of twenty-three and my mother had me at twenty-three. My grandfather was eighteen and my grandmother was seventeen when they married. My mother and her siblings were each two years apart beginning with Herbert, Ruth Ann, Barbara Jean, Tommie Jr., and Dorothy Nell.

My grandparents, Tom (Tommie) and Emma Cline were both from Lockhart, Texas. Lockhart is a small country town. It reminds me of those western movies that included old homes and dusty roads. My mother spent her childhood in Lockhart, but her teen years were in San Antonio where she met my dad.

My grandfather was tall and slim. He was over six feet. A giant next to my grandmother. His skin was a darker hue but not real dark. My cousin Michael looks just like my grandfather, except Michael is light skinned. My grandfather had high cheekbones and he had a softer, thin hair texture. My entire family inherited my grandfather's cheekbones. My aunt Ruth Ann and mother also had his hair texture.

My grandfather and dad could drink, but just like my dad, my grandfather played an active part in his children's lives as well as his grandchildren's. He loved all his grandchildren. He gave my cousin Roselyn the nickname Scooter when she was a baby because instead of crawling on the floor, she would always scoot. She was *his* Scooter. I'd never heard that word until my grandfather nicknamed my cousin. Country people's language, culture, and superstitions are so unique.

My grandfather had this one superstition about using a broom. When we would sweep with our straw broom, if we accidentally swept someone's feet, he'd take the broom and spit on it. Sometimes he'd spit on it even when we didn't sweep anybody's feet. We would say, "Eww, Granddaddy spit on the broom." We thought it was so gross when he did it. He and my mother were also superstitious of black cats. They said that if a black cat crossed your path, then you would have to turn around and never cross the same path because it was bad luck. Or if you were walking with someone and you saw a pole, no one could "split the pole." You'd both have to walk the same way around the pole. If you split up to go around the pole, it was bad luck. If you broke a mirror, it was seven years of bad luck. My grandfather's superstition was passed down to my mother. They both had a country culture to the core. But what we didn't think was country, superstitious, or gross was my grandfather's silver dollars. Naw, we loved them. Every time he would visit us, he would give us all silver dollars. I don't know where he got those silver dollars from, but he always had them and would give them to all his grandchildren. We'd look at the silver dollars and be amazed at how it was a *dollar* but looked similar to an oversized quarter. As soon as he would give them to us, we'd go right to the store and buy candy. We loved when our grandparents visited because we knew we were going to get a silver dollar from my grandfather. They would visit my mother before going fishing and we couldn't wait to get our silver dollars.

My grandparents loved fishing just as much as my parents and it was instilled in us too, passing from generation to generation. They would drive up in their beige car in front of the house when we lived on F Street with their bamboo sticks hanging out of the car window. They would be on their way to fish but make a quick stop to visit my mother. It seemed like my grandfather always had to come check on my mother, especially after my parents separated. My grandfather never liked Alfred. He knew about the constant arguments and even warned my mother that *Alfred was going to rob her out of a house and a home.* He didn't want her with him. My mother wanted her dad to like Alfred, but he didn't. When he'd come to visit, I don't remember Granddaddy ever talking to him or wanting him in the same room. I knew my mom was torn between Alfred and her beloved dad.

My mom talked about both of her parents with endearment, but the one thing she didn't like about her father was the way he treated her mother. It reminded me of the way I didn't approve of how my dad treated my mother, but I still loved him to death. My mom was the same way. She loved her father. I often thought about how conflicting it was to love a father who mistreated your mother. Children always want their fathers to love their mothers and do right by them. I was no different. It was his actions that I hated, not him as a person. I supposed my mother felt the same way I did. Her beloved father took ill not too long after my parents separated. My grandfather was diagnosed with lung cancer in 1978. My uncle bought them a house on Yucca Street, located on the east side of town. It was a few streets away from F Street and Morning View, where my parents lived before the separation, and Dorie Street where Ruth Ann owns her home.

My grandfather was a heavy smoker and always had a cough, but as kids, we didn't know anything about *cancer*. We didn't even understand death at that time. I was nine years old and all I knew was that my grandfather had cancer. I knew that cigarettes caused cancer because of the warning label. I always wondered why my grandfather wouldn't stop smoking if they

37

caused cancer. I used to see him lying on the checkerboard-colored sofa in his home smoking cigarettes and coughing. He'd cough up a lot of mucus and spit it out. He was always a thin man, but with the cancer he was dropping even more weight. My grandfather was stubborn, and he wasn't giving up his Pall Mall cigarettes or his alcohol. He used to buy tobacco and roll his own cigarettes. When he did, it looked just like a joint. Either way, he wasn't going to stop smoking. He also wasn't taking any chemotherapy. He said no doctor was going to kill him! He didn't believe in surgery and medicines despite his daughter Dorothy Nell being a Licensed Vocational Nurse. He was very adamant about his stance on chemotherapy. He still carried the heartbreak of his mother Annie Mae Williams's death.

My grandfather's mother was a Cherokee Indian who was real dark skinned with straight coal black hair. I never knew my grandfather's father, and I don't know how my great-grandmother died. She was seventeen years old when she was first married, and she owned her own land. Her parents were from Alabama. She died when she was fifty-five and my grandfather was thirteen years old. Her death left an invisible scar on him. His distrust of doctors may have stemmed from his mother's death.

It was December of 1979 and I was ten years old. Terrie, Mama, Alfred, and I were fishing at the Willow Springs Golf Course located on E. Commerce Street. We often went to the golf course to fish. When Mama, Terrie, or I weren't with Alfred, he would go alone and bring home big catfish or bass to cook and eat.

On this particular day, I remember it kept drizzling off and on. In Texas it wasn't always cold in winter months. We were waiting under the bridge for the rain to stop so we could continue fishing, but since the weather was murky, instead of staying to fish, we decided to call it a day and return home with the fish we caught. We arrived around evening time and it seemed like we weren't home more than an hour before Mama received a phone call that her father had passed away. She was stunned, but no tears came out. I could only remember my mother crying when my dad left. She handled the death of her father very well. My grandfather's death wasn't unexpected because he had lung cancer. Nevertheless, my beloved grandfather was deceased.

I like to think back to the exact day and time he died and what we were doing. When my grandfather took his last breath, we were under the bridge waiting for the rain to cease. We were giving him permission to go ahead and let go. My mother and her kids would be all right. But maybe he knew it was the calm before the storm and he wouldn't be around to protect my mother.

We traveled to my grandfather's hometown of Lockhart, Texas to bury him. I wore a peach dress with white ruffles around the collar. It was a dress that my aunt had gave to me from my cousin, Roselyn. My aunt often brought my sister and I hand-me-down clothes, but they were always like new and in excellent condition. I couldn't wait until Dorothy Nell brought those big Hefty trash bags full of clothes for me to wear. It was like Christmas Day for Terrie and me. Terrie wore a burgundy pinstripe skirt set from the clothes that were given to us, and my mother pressed our hair and combed it alike. She made sure that we looked nice for her father's funeral.
The service was all a blur to me, but I remember not knowing many of my relatives from Lockhart and that my family and I felt very left out. My aunt Ruth Ann and other cousins frequented Lockhart almost monthly, so they knew all our kin

folks. I remember my aunt going out with Julia Faye and my mother refusing to go with them. She stayed with Alfred and her kids.

We didn't stay long in Lockhart. After my grandfather was buried, we drove back home to San Antonio.
In the car, we played music. Rhythm and Blues, but I don't remember much conversation between us. We wanted to get home to a familiar place since we felt like outsiders in Lockhart. The eerie ghost stories that my mother always told made the small town even spookier. Like a ghost town full of dead people buried everywhere.

My grandpa was the first person in our family to die. I didn't know what death was, but I felt robbed. I would never see my grandfather again. He would never spit on the broom, or give us silver dollars, or come visit and give us unconditional love. He'd never call my cousin Roselyn *Scooter*. My granddaddy passing away was when I realized how unfair life was. He was gone too soon.

Rest in peace, Granddaddy. Rest assured that you will live on through my words.

Tommie (T.C.) Cline
July 22, 1922 - December 28, 1979

Chapter Nine

My First Love

*E*very little girl has a first love, and I was no different from the rest, except the boy I loved never liked or saw me as a love interest. It has never ceased to amaze me how boys that you like don't like you back, and when boys like you, you don't like them. How and why was this law of attraction even fair?

I was twelve years old when I realized I liked my neighbor Allen's cousin. He frequented Allen's house almost every weekend, but in the summer, it was more than once a week. Connie was his name and he was one year older than me. He lived on the east side of town in the Dellcrest subdivision. His parents owned a home and his mother worked for the phone company. My mother went to school with his father. Connie was a junior named after his father.

I loved, loved me some Connie. I don't know exactly why, but I did. Connie was skinny with brown skin and light-colored eyes. He was a little taller than me but not much. He had a younger brother named Michael. Tomboy that I was, I only got next to him when I raced him down the streets of Bethune. He and I often raced to see who was the fastest. I can't remember who won but we were always put against one another. Maybe I was the winner and the reason he never had any interest in me? I never told him that he was my crush, but Allen knew I had the hots for Connie, so I'm sure he heard. One thing I learned in life was: if you like a guy, don't tell any of your *girl*friends because they will find him attractive as well. I told Ms. Bettie's daughter Tina who was the same age as Connie that I liked him, and from that day forward, she began liking him too.

Allen had a birthday party and he was turning seventeen. He was my brother's friend and they often hung out together. Allen invited Tina and Edward to his house party but didn't invite *me*. I told my brother to ask Allen if I could go because I wanted to get closer to Connie. Allen told my brother that only thirteen and up could attend his party. Thirteen and up? I was only twelve, so I was devastated. Not only couldn't I attend, but my friend Tina was old enough to go and I wasn't. I was so upset at Allen, who nicknamed me "Slim" because I was so skinny and could run fast, but I couldn't stand him from that day forward since he didn't let me attend his party. Every time he called me "Slim" I rolled my eyes. Tina was invited to the party, and of course Connie was there too. I told Tina to watch her every move to make sure she didn't get next to him. My sister obliged.

The party was held in Allen's backyard facing our backyard. There were over fifty school kids, friends, and family in attendance. Night came, and my mother and I sat on the back porch to watch the party as I cried inside, watching them dance and play music. The Dazz Band, "You Dropped the Bomb on Me" and "Let It Whip" stole the night as I watched Allen's sister Sheba dance. She tore up every dance move with her plaid ruffled-in-the-front blouse that was *very* popular during that time, and her skin-tight blue jeans that hugged her body so nicely. I was mesmerized by Sheba and so was my mother. The only good thing about that night was she kept my mind off Connie. I hardly saw him and when I did my attention was drawn back to Sheba and her dance moves.

The party ended early because a jealous neighbor called the police for music being played too loud. It was the Sutton Homes, the ghetto. Whoever heard of the police coming to shut a party down in the ghetto? Allen and his family were upset, and since Connie's mother worked for the phone company, she was going to find out who called the police based on the phone records. I don't know if they ever found out who called, but I wasn't mad at that person because I wanted Tina away from Connie anyway.

Connie went to school with my cousin, Roselyn. They were in the same grade. I told her about him and how much I liked him. But it all came crashing down after that.

We were at vacation Bible study during the summer when I was staying with her over the break. My aunt always had us going to church. She would give us money to put in the offering. When she'd drop us off at church, we would go to Sunday school, and once it ended we would frequent the neighborhood corner store located on Martin Luther King Drive and take our money to play video games. My aunt didn't know we were doing this until one day we actually went to church after Sunday school and my cousin Roselyn caught the Holy Ghost spirit. Since she caught the "Holy Ghost," she no longer wanted to skip church and play video games. She told my aunt what we were doing. We got in trouble and no longer skipped church to play video games. But one day before my cousin caught the Holy Ghost, we were in Vacation Bible School when she pulled me to the side and asked me if I still liked Connie. I didn't know why she asked when she knew I did. Then for some reason, I told her I didn't. She said good because she'd kissed him at school. *What? You kissed my Connie?* My heart broke into pieces when she told me that she'd kissed *my* Connie. My first love. I could no longer look at him the same way after he kissed my cousin. I got over him quickly.

43

Connie no longer interested me, so I turned my attention to an older boy that lived in my aunt's apartment complex. He was so handsome and fine. He was more mature and better looking than Connie. His smile was amazing. His name was Garland Woods and he was the brother of a girl named Stephanie that I went to school with. Stephanie and I were in cheerleading and played sports together. But her brother Garland was out of my league since he was four years older than me and had a girlfriend. It never stopped me from admiring him. I often watched him like a hawk, coming and going from his apartment.

A few years later, I met a boy from the Sutton Homes named Terry. Terry was dark brown with a thick afro, but it looked like he used some hair products to make it soft and curly. It was still thick but had a curl texture to it. I really liked Terry and of course I hadn't learned to keep my mouth closed about boys that I was interested in. I told my best friend Nickki about Terry since she didn't live too far from him. We were fourteen years old and in high school.

One night, Terry had a house party, but it wasn't his birthday. Back in those days, everybody was always throwing house parties, but Terry didn't invite me to this party. It was his brother who said I could come.

I arrived late and it was real dark inside the house. I saw a lot of teenagers slow dancing to the song "Slow Jam" by Midnight Star. I couldn't make out faces because the lights were off and only an outside light was glaring through a window. I walked around and got something to drink. I got some chips too. There wasn't much of anything left.

I saw a couple slow dancing and grinding to the music. The guy looked just like Terry. I walked closer to them because I needed to know if it was him or not. My feet were moving in slow motion the closer I got to the couple and my heart began to flutter. I was within inches of them when I recognized him because of his hair; it was Terry slow dancing with my friend Nickki! Her head was resting on his shoulder and her eyes were closed. She was grinding on *my* Terry! Neither one of them saw me as I thought to myself: *Oh no, not again. First my cousin with Connie, and now my best friend with Terry.*

I watched for two seconds longer and then I left unnoticed. I hated the song "Slow Jam" from that day forward because it reminded me of the betrayal. It was the end of my crush on Terry, not only because he was with my best friend, but after Tina told my mother about my crush on him, Mama said I couldn't have any boyfriends until I finished high school.

I did what my mother said; I never had any boyfriends. And Connie, who I thought was my first love? He wasn't— that was my father. My dad left when I was eight years old and moved in with Rose. He broke our family apart in the process, and from that day forward I *never* trusted men. My father remained faithful to Rose and Della, his mistresses. What made him constantly cheat on my mother would remain a mystery that only he could answer.

Chapter Ten

There Goes Grandmama

*M*y father's relationship with Della was stable. I don't know if he really loved her or not. I think he just settled since he left Mama and then tried to reconcile a few years after he left. Mama turned him down and went on with her life with her new man, Alfred. Dad and Della remained a couple. Della with her three kids, and my dad's four.

My father's mother was moving from her house on Fargo Street into a rough neighborhood called the East Terrace. She would be living in the housing projects, but the area she was moving to was specifically for the elderly. My grandmother was sixty-nine years old when she moved. I remember my father being adamant about her not moving but I guess he lost the battle.

We visited her often and did some of the same family outings as when she lived on Fargo Street. Whenever my father visited, he'd take us along with him. Even though my parents were separated (they never divorced), we were always with our father. He never left us. He took us everywhere he went except to work. And when we knew he was off work, we would tell him to pick us up early from school and he'd always oblige.

I remember one day when I was in fifth grade, my father came to get me out of school early. I knew he was coming because we had already made plans. When he came to Mrs. Hastings's class to get me, my teacher asked for his ID even though he had already checked in with the office before he got to the classroom. I thought it was odd for her to ask this since I'd never seen her do it to other students' parents when they picked their children up early. And then it dawned on me that I looked nothing like my father, and I understood why she asked. My sister Tina looked exactly like my father and grandmother, Mamie. If you put a wig on Tina, then you would be looking at my grandmother. That's how much they looked alike.

When we'd visit my grandmother, my aunt Pauline would sometimes be there from California. She'd frequent my grandmother's place often and each time she came to San Antonio, she'd ask my sister embarrassing questions in front of everyone, like: "Tina Lynn, are you still a virgin?"

Then she'd ask about my sister's menstruation.

Tina would answer but it annoyed me hearing my aunt ask such *personal* questions. I don't remember my dad telling his sister anything. My aunt Pauline was bold and very fat. She weighed over 300 pounds and she used to breathe heavily. She was my dad's oldest sister and she lived until she was eighty.

Pauline didn't have any children that I could remember, but she kept tabs on my sister as if she was her child instead of her niece. My grandmother never asked my sister any of her personal business. She treated us all with respect and often gave us coins and peppermint candies. She let us run around her house and get whatever we wanted from the refrigerator without saying a word. Just like my father, my grandmother never got after us about anything, and we all enjoyed visiting her with my father. She was a big part of our lives growing up. She used to go fishing with us quite often. And she'd always fish with bamboo sticks.

We used balled-up bread mixed with vanilla extract and wieners for bait. My grandmother used to spit on the bait before she threw her bamboo stick in the water. She'd always

47

catch perches and she'd keep them all, no matter how big or small. She loved to fish.

My family had a history of fishing. When my parents were together, we loved going to Brauning and Calavares Lakes. We'd go to Three Rivers and catch Jaws. That's where the big fish were. We had many fishing areas that we frequented. But one time our family outing didn't last long before something tragic happened.

It was my brother's birthday, July 8, 1984.

We went to my grandmother's house and saw yellow crime tape draped across her apartment door. I was fourteen years old. Instead of celebrating my brother's birthday, we were at my grandma's house with news cameras and the police department. A murder investigation was taking place right before my eyes. I saw a stretcher with a body covered in a white sheet being carried out of my grandmother's home. It was a huge body that was tied down with blue straps and the face was covered. My grandmother was a short medium size woman.

We weren't allowed to go inside the apartment, so we were outside talking and that's when we saw my cousin Ronnie crying. He was crying hard and it was unlike him since he never cried.

I looked inside my grandmother's house and I saw two black handprints on the bathroom door and the window was broken. I was young and couldn't comprehend everything that had taken place.

It was the middle of the night when my grandmother heard a knock on her front door. She got up to answer and it was an unknown woman. She didn't know her, so she didn't open the door. During the time she was at the front door being distracted by the knock, she heard glass breaking. She went to see where the noise came from and that's when she saw a man trying to get inside her bathroom window. The man got in, overpowered her, and unlocked the front door to let the woman inside. While inside my grandmother's apartment, they demanded money, but she wouldn't tell them where it was. My grandmother was retired, and she was frugal and saved all of her money. Since she wouldn't give them what they wanted, they began beating her. The intruders held her down and suffocated my grandma with a pillow. She'd only lived in the East Terrace for a short time, but my dad's fear of her moving to the projects had come to fruition. My father didn't cry; he just walked around in a daze. We couldn't believe that our beloved grandmother was robbed and brutally murdered. She was seventy years old.

My aunt Debra made the funeral arrangements and my grandmother was buried in a coffin that looked like cement. It was a hideous casket and I wondered why she was buried so cheaply when she had insurance policies that could afford her the best. My grandmother saved and took care of important business such as life insurance policies. She'd mentioned it before, and I saw a stack of important papers that she kept locked away. As kids, we made all types of assumptions about how the intruders knew that my grandmother had money, and who murdered her. We even blamed my aunt.
Fortunately, the crime was solved through Crime Stoppers. The police found the people responsible for my grandmother's death and they went to prison.

We were bad kids growing up and often made fun of my grandmother when she heard her favorite Blues song. After she passed away, we continued to be bad by scaring each other with grandma jokes. We all shared a room together and slept in the same king size bed. We slept two at the top of the bed and two at the bottom.

One time my brother had chicken pox and no one wanted to sleep at the same end as him. We would make fun and tease him. My poor brother caught hell for being the only boy in the family. No one would sleep at the same end with him. I felt bad so I reluctantly slept next to him.

We had this dresser with a mirror and each night before going to bed, we'd cover the mirror with a sheet so that we wouldn't see Grandmama. We knew she was dead, but we didn't want her to haunt us, so each night we'd throw the sheet over the mirror. One night, we forgot to put the sheet over the mirror, so Tina looked in the mirror and told us, "There go Grandmama."

We looked in the mirror without the sheet and began laughing. We didn't want to get up and throw the sheet on the mirror because we were scared. We've always played the "There go Grandmama" game since her death. We were bad. We didn't understand death.

Rest in peace, Grandma.
Mamie D. Campbell
April 1, 1914 - July 8, 1984

Chapter Eleven

Daddy Cry

A month and a half after we buried our grandmother, life wasn't the same for my father. He never verbally expressed that something was wrong with him; he just kept pushing through life. His mother was a constant in all our lives, and she was missed.

The same year my grandmother passed away, my brother decided he was no longer going to school. He'd hated school with a passion ever since he was small. He was sixteen years old and had repeated several grades. I caught up with him when he was supposed to be in my ninth-grade biology class, but he never showed. My brother quitting school brought our father to our home. He wasn't allowed inside, but this was the first time I had ever seen him within fifty feet of the door. My mother didn't want him anywhere around her. She never interfered with his relationship with us, he could see us whenever he wanted, and he did.

Dad came to our home to try and convince my brother to go back to school. It was important for all his children to get an education. He stressed this often growing up and it was the reason he made certain my brother was first to show his report card. Daddy didn't play when it came to education.

I will never forget my dad standing in front of our house with tears in his eyes when he found out my brother wasn't returning to school. He never cried at his mother's funeral or about her death. But my brother brought him to tears. My dad quit school in the eleventh grade, and based on my father's reaction to the news that my brother wasn't going to finish, it could have been one of his greatest regrets. My father told him that if he didn't want to go to school then he needed to get a job. He wanted to make sure that he made something out of his life. He refused to let my brother fail.

My brother worked with my dad and uncle Tommie doing construction work. When my brother got paid on Fridays, he would go out with his friends and didn't want to work the next day. He purchased Michael Jackson's infamous Thriller jacket and parachute pants that were very popular in those days. My dad and brother would get into arguments because my brother would get paid and didn't want to work. This was a constant battle between the two of them. When my dad and brother weren't arguing over my brother being a responsible young man, he, my brother, and my cousin James would go to the basketball court and shoot hoops.

My dad was maybe five foot eight, but he loved playing basketball with the younger guys. He was in his late thirties, but he could keep up with them. He was always active. He'd play football with us in front of his house. I'd be right there with him because he was the reason I loved football so much. Any opportunity I got, I wanted my dad's attention, affection, and love. He was the reason I'd strive so hard in school. I knew my father's interests and I catered to them, and my dad catered to his girls. He put Tina, Terrie, and me before everyone else. We were all his favorites because Daddy loved all his children. But it hurt me so bad that I wasn't his biological child and looked nothing like him.

When I was sixteen years old and was over at his house for the summer, Della's son Quincy had an Atari game, and we'd play that game from sunup to sundown. I'd visit my crush, Rodney, when my father was at work. But when he was home, I'd take time away from Atari and Rodney, and put baby oil all over my body and sit outside in the sunlight.

One day my dad caught me outside in the sun and asked what I was doing. I told him nothing, but I was outside in the sun trying to make my skin darker. I wanted to look like my dad and siblings. He'd tell me to come inside.

"Tammy, it's too hot to be out here."

"Daddy, I'll be inside in a minute."

That minute never came, and he'd come back outside looking for me. I was still out there, but I had moved to another area so that he couldn't see me. He'd find me again to get me out of the sun. It reminded me of many times when I was about nine years old. I would hide under my bed when it was school time, and my mother would be looking for me, but I'd just lay there quietly. It wasn't until she said that she was going to call the police that I'd come out of hiding. I don't know why I loved to hide when I was younger.

I didn't want to tell my dad that I was trying to look like him or how much it affected me that he wasn't my biological father. I kept all the hurt and pain inside me. I desperately wanted him to be my *real* dad. I'd do anything for him to be. If I'd had one wish, it would've been to look like him. I tried everything to make my skin darker. When prayers didn't work, I got the baby oil. I'd get a shade darker for the summer but nothing close to my father's complexion. My original skin color would return in autumn. The darker I tried to become, the more ugly pimples I got on my face with all the baby oil clogging my pores, not to mention teenage hormones. Those hormones were taking a toll on me in addition to my identity crisis. I was going into the eleventh grade, and not only did I want to change my complexion, I wanted the latest hairstyle too. The infamous Jheri Curl. I begged my daddy for a Jheri Curl, a *Wave Nouveau*.

It was about sixty-five dollars to have the Wave Nouveau professionally done at a beauty shop. Terrie and I never had any kind of chemicals on our hair. My mother was the only person to straighten and wash it. Tina would braid and plait it sometimes, but she and my mom were the only ones allowed to do our hair. I don't know if my father found the lady that lived near him, or if I was the one who got information that she did Jheri Curls and only charged thirty dollars. My dad told us to ask my mother if we could get Jheri Curls and he would pay for them. Terrie and I got permission from my mother and we went to get our hair done. My father dropped us off at the lady's house on Saturday after his payday. He'd return to pick us up once she was finished.

Before the lady began, she asked if we ever had any relaxers or chemicals in our hair. We told her, "no." She kept saying that my sister's and my hair was "virgin" hair. We didn't understand what she meant but she kept telling the people that visited while we were getting the Jheri Curls that we had "virgin" hair.

Terrie's hair had always come out better than mine because it was black and held a really nice shine. My hair was sandy dark brown and dull. My curl didn't come out the way it looked on the curl box nor how I envisioned it. But I couldn't tell my dad that I didn't like it. He paid his hard-earned money to make us happy so I couldn't hurt his feelings. The way I felt about my hair had nothing to do with my father but had everything to do with how I saw myself. I didn't hate me. I just didn't like the fact that I looked nothing like the people I loved most in life; my family. Everyone accepted and loved me as me. I was the one with the issues. I wanted Daddy to say something about my complexion, but he never did. I looked in the mirror and had a light skin complex. I loved myself, but hated my skin color. Daddy never knew how much I cried because I didn't look like him. No one knew. It was my Daddy Cry.

Chapter Twelve

Generational Curse

*M*y identity was one problem among many. I didn't realize how many issues I could have at such a young age. Who says young people don't have problems? I vehemently disagree—now let me explain.

Early morning arguments, whether it was a school night, or not, were a constant. The foul language played like a favorite song that you hated but couldn't stop listening to. A scratched 45-inch vinyl spinning on the record player. Why couldn't somebody stop or turn it off? I had to go to school in the morning.

"Fuck you, bitch! You can't have no kids. You're too old for me."

I remember the exact disrespectful words spewed like poisonous venom at my mother. And Mama talking her shit back at him, but I don't remember her response. All I knew was, words did hurt because my self-esteem sank six feet into an unmarked grave. I'm sure Mama's was already there.

How dare a low-life bum talk to my mother like that? Who does he think he is? I spoke silently to myself as I got out of bed to go in the closet and cover my ears to drown out the voices. This wasn't what I signed up for, and neither had Mama when Alfred *promised* that he would take care of us after Daddy left. That promise fell by the wayside just as fast as we packed our things and moved back to Sutton Homes. The ghetto.

This wasn't the first argument between Mama and Alfred, nor was it the last. It was *years* before Mama's family convinced her to leave him. Eight years to be exact. A long time. Too long.

Daddy's absence was more apparent as I heard the words "bitch" and "whore" continuously. The vinyl record kept spinning for hours. Yes, hours. I never understood how someone could argue for hours. When I went to my dad's house I never heard him and Della argue. I'm sure they did, but not when I was around. And certainly not in the middle of the morning. What had Mama gotten herself and her kids into? I prayed every day for her to leave Alfred's because she deserved better. If only she could've realized it. I'm sure she knew, but he was the only one who worked. He was the breadwinner, or rather the *crumb winner,* because that's what he brought home. Crumbs. And sometimes he didn't even bring them home. Mama was caught between a rock and a hard place. She stayed because it was more convenient than being alone. Her self-esteem was long gone even before she met Alfred or Daddy. She did what her mother did. Accepted the abuse. The generational curse was passed along like a flowing river.

Chapter Thirteen

Turnaround Country

F ox Tech High School, the home where the Buffaloes roamed. A place where I spent four of my teenage years before I transitioned into adulthood.

I was leaving Emerson Middle School. If I could've stayed an Emerson Bobcat forever, I would have. Middle school was my pride and joy, especially being the captain of the cheerleading team. My love for cheering never died. But my dream of being a Buffalo cheerleader in high school did. Living in poverty was no joke. We couldn't even afford to be poor. That's how poor we were. I couldn't afford to be a Bobcat cheerleader, so I never asked Mama about becoming a Buffalo cheerleader. Those uniforms cost an arm and a leg, and we didn't have a pot to pee in.

I was so jealous of the cheerleaders, but one girl in particular, named Shalisa. She wasn't an Emerson Bobcat cheerleader, so I don't know why she tried out and made the Buffalo cheer team. But for some reason it irked me that she joined the squad.
I must have rolled my eyes until they almost fell out watching her at the pep rallies cheering. Not only was she a cheerleader, she was also an "A" student.

That was a double unfair whammy. *Bam!*

I wanted and needed to be out there near the cheerleaders, so I did whatever it took to get next to the cheer squad. My friend Lottie and I joined the flag team.

Lottie and I stayed after school to practice, and on the first day, we must have dropped that flag until it needed mouth-to-mouth resuscitation. I tried to spin it between my petite fingers and couldn't get it through them all. Then I tried to twirl it over my head, and I popped myself in the face. It wasn't working for me, so my friend and I quit the flag team. We didn't last a week.

But the fight with the flag didn't deter me. I had to think of another plan to get next to those cheerleaders, so Lottie and I joined the Fox Tech band. We were in the ninth grade. Neither one of us played an instrument. My friend Tonya played the flute and I always admired her, so I played the same instrument. Lottie played the clarinet. Throughout the school year, we both excelled in our respective instruments. We were in a beginner's band, but we played so well that the band director, Mr. Ross, let us play along with the advanced band. Finally, I was set to get next to the cheerleaders.

One day, Lottie and I were playing with the advanced band. The flutes always sat in the first row and clarinets sat in the row behind us. We had a small intermission and I turned around to talk to Lottie. Our teacher was ready to begin again, but I ignored him until I was done talking. I didn't finish until I heard Mr. Ross yell at the top of his lungs, "Turn around, Country!" A nickname he gave me from day one when he called the roll and I answered, "Present."

Instead of calling me Tammy, he'd say, "Country" and the class would burst out laughing. I hated when he called me Country, but he loved teasing me. He couldn't believe I was from San Antonio because he thought I had a "country" accent.

Lottie was his favorite among us. He never got after her, and in fact, she was the reason he offered us a place in the parade. He wanted us to join the band along with the cheerleaders in the San Antonio Fiesta parade! Was he kidding me? We couldn't say yes fast enough— except we weren't going to play our instruments like we thought. Nope! He wanted us to carry the Fox Tech Banner. Carry the banner? Huh? What? Was he serious? How dare Mr. Ross insult our instrumental talent by asking us to carry the banner.
We couldn't believe him. But yeah, we went ahead and carried that banner. I mean, we were leading the parade!

The patrons stood clapping and dancing to the sound of each high school band that passed their way. When we passed East Houston and Commerce Street by the post office, our friends that knew us from Sutton Homes yelled our names like we were superstars. We were well known. We waved and smiled back while Mr. Ross gave me a look that said "you need to behave" because I kept dancing and showing my tail. I was shaking my little booty in my white pants and red shirt, the colors of Fox Tech. But I clearly wanted to do more dancing than anything, so his look warned me—I was there to *carry the banner*.

Lottie and I didn't get to display our instrumental talent to the world that day, but Mr. Ross gave us an opportunity to shine. By carrying the banner, we shined brighter than those cheerleaders and band instruments!

Chapter Fourteen

The Jeffersons

*O*ur parade debut didn't last long, and Lottie and I didn't pursue band the next year. We were done playing instruments and carrying banners, but it was fun while it lasted. During the same year I played in the band, I was also involved in volleyball. I continued the same sports from Emerson Middle School to Fox Tech until I had a disagreement with my coach.

I wasn't a great volleyball player, but I wasn't bad either. I played in every game even though I wouldn't always start. I was probably the sixth or seventh player coming off the bench when I didn't start. I stayed after school each day to practice, not only with the freshman team, but we would also practice against the junior varsity and varsity teams.

There was this one girl who was a good server and her balls were hard and fast. She'd serve the ball so hard that many of us would let the ball go by because we didn't want it to sting our arms. The coach used to have her serve to the freshmen team. This was a constant grind on our arms, but it was *supposed* to make us better. It was more like abuse from an upperclassman. I hated the serving drills, but I did them because I'm a team player. I put a lot of effort into volleyball and my coach played me during each game. Since I had an active role on the team, I invited my family to come watch me play. I had been asking and begging them to come see me play, so when they finally agreed I was elated. I wanted to show them what I could do on the volleyball court.

My family arrived at the game and I greeted them with a smile, going to the bleachers to talk to them before the game. I was so excited to see them. I played many sports and cheered for many games at Emerson Middle School, but this was the *first* time that my family ever came to one of my events. I was going to show them what I had.

My greatest strength was my defense. My serve was decent, but I could play well enough to be on the court. When the game began, I was on the bench. This wasn't a big deal because sometimes I started and sometimes I didn't. As the game went on, though, I noticed some of my teammates who never played in the games getting an opportunity for playing time. I thought to myself, *maybe their family came to see them play and they asked to be put into the game.* I sat there watching. I'd look up into the bleachers at my family and their expressions seemed to say, "why aren't you getting in the game? I thought you said you were good?" The looks on their faces intensified my frustration the more the game went on and I was still on the bench. I had begged them to come to my game only to see me riding the bench. I was happy they didn't tease me about it and were just as disappointed as me. I wasted their time, and my coach wasted mine. I sat on the bench but I couldn't wait until the game ended. I was going to give my coach a piece of my mind. I couldn't believe she hadn't put me in the game. I was livid.

The game ended and I never got an opportunity to play. This was so odd because I had always played in every game. I asked my family to wait for me because I was going to talk to the coach. I walked to the coach and asked her if I could talk to her. I wanted to talk to her *right then.* She embarrassed me in front of my family and she was going to hear about it. She agreed and knew I was upset. We went out the back doors of the gym and that's when I let her have it!

I told her how hard I practiced, pointed out how I always played, and explained that the one time my family came to see me all I did was sit on the bench. And then I said, "I could have been at home watching the *Jeffersons!*" I told her I didn't have time for that shit! And then I walked off and quit the volleyball team. She embarrassed and humiliated me in front of my family. They didn't come to the game to see me riding the bench.

I didn't play any more high school sports after that because many of the high school coaches taught multiple sports. I wanted to run track, but the volleyball coach was also the track and field coach. My love for the hurdles didn't die, but the regret of not running track in high school still hurts. I was one of the greatest hurdlers in middle school. And if my coach hadn't benched me in front of my family during that volleyball game, I could have been greater at the hurdles in high school. My pride played a major role in what happened the day I gave my volleyball coach a piece of my mind. From that day forward, I went straight home every day and watched my favorite after school TV show, the *Jeffersons*.

On weekends, there was a neighborhood wife and husband that had a small business and would take teenage kids to sell candy and make a profit.

I learned about the "candy man" from my friend Lottie, who used to sell candy too. We sold all types of candy. Mints, peanut brittle, peanut patties, and sometimes bean pies. They made some delicious bean pies and I still can't find any like the ones they made. The husband and wife were Muslims, and each time we'd get inside the candy van on our way to sell candy we'd have to greet them and each other with "*As-Salaam-Alaikum,*" meaning, "peace unto you." If they said it to us first, we would respond with, "*wa ʿalaykumu s-salām,*" or "peace unto you, too." Muhammad, the husband, would get upset if we forgot the Muslim greeting, so we each had it memorized.

The candy man would pick us up after school on weekends and during the summer months. They used to go out of town and sell as well. I never wanted to travel with them out of town because I didn't want to stay in a hotel room with a lot of kids and I always got strange vibes from the husband, but being a young teenager, I didn't know why. I didn't trust him, and most of the time I stayed with his wife Fatima when it came to my candy routes. Fatima was a soft spoken, spirited lady that wore a hijab on top of her head. She was a submissive woman and did whatever her husband asked of her. They had about four small children at that time who were often with us when we sold candy.

One day I was out selling candy and I saw this white man in a window facing the street I was walking down. I asked him if he wanted to buy any candy. He told me that he couldn't hear me and told me to come closer, so I walked closer to his window. I noticed as I got closer and closer that he wasn't wearing a shirt. He continued saying that he couldn't hear me until I stood right next to the window and looked into his big blue eyes. He looked like a deer caught in the headlights, but I continued to ask if he wanted to buy any candy. He didn't say anything, he just kept looking at me with a weird smile like he was concentrating on something else. It seemed sinister and demonic. His silence made me look at his lower body because his arm was moving, and that's when my eyes followed his moving arm and I saw that he was naked and masturbating. I picked up my candy and took off running. He seemed to think it was funny because he laughed out loud while I ran. I told Fatima about the incident and she warned us girls that we needed to sell candy as partners and not to leave each other alone. The man scared me. I can still see his face, his big blue eyes, his penis, his wet hairy chest and body like he just got out of the shower. And I can hear his laugh.

What I didn't know was the man, Muhammad, who I sold candy for, was no different than the man I ran away from that day.

It was on every news station in San Antonio Texas, in 1984. I was fourteen years old and I learned about it from a friend I sold candy with. I knew the victims and the victimizer. Muhammad, who we called the "candy man," was arrested on charges of sexual assault against minors. On the out of town trips they took selling candy, he was in hotel rooms molesting and having sex with underage girls. I was shocked, but not surprised. I had always felt some uneasiness when I was around Mr. Muhammad. I never went around him without his wife being present.

There were a lot of grown men peeping and looking at teenage girls when I was growing up. They were pitiful, sick souls, with issues, too.

Chapter Fifteen

Role Models

I was a child way ahead of my time. My maturity level began at a young age, analyzing my parents as well as other relationships around me. It was like I was immune to everything that was negative and rarely saw things that would instill what was a healthy and satisfying relationship. I had seen and endured so much in such a small amount of time on this earth. It was a disappointment to say the least to see the world the way it was, but I had quite a few female role models around me and each one played a massive part in shaping me into the woman I am today. I'm not perfect, and neither were my role models, but they were always there for me, through thick and thin.

My mother's side of the family were very close. My aunts and uncles were there to support each other. Unfortunately, my mother needed the most support financially, and even though my aunts and uncles had their own families to take care of, they were always there to lend a hand to my mom. I loathed needing so much assistance from others, but I had no control over anything at that time. I was helpless and hopeless, but determined. I made a promise to myself that when I become old enough to work, I wouldn't ask anyone for a dime. I didn't like pity, or anyone thinking of us as, "Bobbie Jean and her poor kids." Each time my aunts and uncles provided for us, that was the feeling that resonated. I could hardly wait to turn sixteen and get a real job so I could take care of myself. I wanted to get my mother as far away from the ghetto and poverty as I could. It was my dream to do so by going into the Air Force as soon as I graduated. But that was only a distant goal.

When I was fourteen, there was a paper company that resided next to us in the Sutton Homes and I always envisioned myself working there, making "big bucks," and taking care of Mama. I wanted to give my mom a break from all the hard work and struggle she had gone through in her marriage and raising four children. I thought about how I was going to get out of poverty often when I was young. I didn't like Mama always having to call and ask her family for food or money. Or the fact that we were in need even without asking. It was an uncomfortable feeling, as though we were the laughingstock or failures of the family. It seemed like everyone had things going for them to make a better life except *us*. My aunts and uncles had their own homes and they even opened a furniture store on W.W. White Rd. The furniture store didn't last long, but nonetheless, they tried. The store was a nice start.

One day at the store my aunt Dorothy Nell sang this nursery rhyme. I don't know if she made it up because I'd never heard it before, but I will never forget her singing:

"My mama told me if I be good, that she would buy me a rubber doll. My sister told her I kissed a soldier now she won't buy me a rubber doll. Now I'm a lady, I have a baby, and I don't need no rubber doll."

She sang to my cousin Cedric because he was the only "baby" at the time. We loved hearing her sing that song. It brought great joy and smiles to our faces.

I considered myself lucky to be raised around my aunt Dorothy Nell. I watched everything she did. She would roll her hair up at night with pink sponge rollers, and in the morning take the rollers out to get ready for work at the Santa Rosa

Hospital. We'd visit her at the hospital sometimes too. I admired that she worked, and thought to myself that when I grew up I was going to be just as dedicated as she was to working and raising her children. She gave my cousins the best of everything that she could. She made it look so easy when I knew that it wasn't. One thing I noticed about my aunt was that she always gave her children her full attention. It didn't matter what they were saying; she was attentive and listened. I don't ever remember her getting upset, or my cousins getting spankings. She never spanked them, but my cousins weren't as bad as my sisters and brother. They had the necessities in life such as food, water, and a better environment. I never envied my cousins, but I knew that when I had children, I was going to raise them the same way as my aunt.

There were times when she was living paycheck to paycheck and I can't imagine how hard it was for her, trying to help my family while raising her own children. She worked hard so that everyone she loved could live comfortably. I know this because I'm the same way she was.

When I was staying with my aunt in the eleventh grade, she took my cousins and me to Windsor Park Mall, let us pick out our own school clothes, and paid for them with her Penney's credit card. I chose a red blouse and some checkered green pants that had a mix of red. I wore red shoes and it was my favorite outfit. I loved it so much that I wore it weekly instead of every other week. I didn't care. I thought I was cute and it was brand new.

My aunt was intelligent; my mother always told me how smart she was.

"Dorothy Nell won't take 'no' for an answer. If you tell her no, she will ask for the manager," my mother bragged. When Mama told me that about my aunt, I decided that I wanted to be just like her and never take "no" for an answer.

I'm the spitting image of my aunt when it comes to taking care of business. She always took care of her business first, and then material things came second or not at all.

My aunt Ruth Ann was the same as Dorothy Nell. She worked hard. She and her husband James were married for over twenty years until his death in 1994. Big James died from cancer. She and James were a middle-class couple that built something out of nothing and were happily married.

My uncle loved to cook. I think he was a chef and worked at Earl Abel's for many years. He loved desserts and baking cakes. When he got off work, he'd sometimes go to Tucker's Lounge or just chill at home. I always wanted a relationship like my aunt Ruth Ann had. She and James would save their money and then go with my uncle Tommie, his wife, and my grandmother to Las Vegas. They were always taking vacations and buying cars.

My aunt's favorite brands of cars were Cadillacs and Lincolns. I've never known her to own anything else. It seemed like she got a new car often and she loved playing her music in them. I remember whenever she got a new car we'd be so excited to get inside and sit in the back seat. We thought she would play music we could dance to. Nope. She'd turn on her *country* music. We couldn't believe my aunt and her music genre. But she knew all the country songs and singers. Her music preference was totally opposite my own. My siblings and I loved soul music, but we knew Kenny Rogers, Dolly Parton, and Willie Nelson from my mom.

My aunt Ruth Ann taught me how to get a man and build with him. No relationship is perfect, but if you work together you can get yourself out of poverty. She worked for years until she retired from Northeast Baptist Hospital.

My grandmothers, Emma and Mamie, were similar, and I learned one valuable lesson from them, which was to keep

70

money hidden. We called it a *stash*. They had money in old purses and shoe boxes—places no one would ever find. They were both frugal, and never broke. My mother used to tell me that I could make a dollar last an entire week. I'd laugh when she would say that, but I learned from both grandmothers. I watched everything that my role models did and I was grateful to have them in my life.

My mother was my greatest role model. She had her flaws like we all do, but she taught me to be resilient and to put your children first. She loved her family, and her life revolved around her kids and my father until the separation. After the marriage ended, she still had us, and there was a saying around the neighborhood: "don't mess with Bobbie Jean's kids."

She kept us clean despite growing up in poverty. We didn't have a washing machine, but we'd get our clothes, put them in the bathtub, and stomp on them with our feet to get them clean. After stomping them, we'd hang them on the clothesline out in the backyard. She made sure we had clean clothes and our hair was combed. My mother fixed my hair until I was in the ninth grade, but she stopped when my friend made a comment about her still fixing it.

We were eating breakfast at school one morning with my sister and my friend Daphonie. I don't know what we were talking about or how the conversation about hair came up, but I stated that my mother combed my hair and she said, "Ooh, yo mama *still* comb your hair?" I didn't see anything wrong with my mom combing my hair. Wasn't it similar to going to the beauty salon and letting someone else fix your hair? I felt embarrassed by her comment, so from that day forward, Tina combed my hair instead of my mother.

I couldn't style hair if my life depended on it. I was challenged in that area. But my sister wasn't. She'd always styled her own hair from an early age, and she experimented on Terrie's and mine often. I don't remember how I told my mom that I no longer wanted her to comb my hair. She did everything for us. I mean everything. She'd even iron our clothes.

She was and will always be my *SHERO*. My number one role model.

Chapter Sixteen

Love

I've always looked for role models. Not in famous celebrities, but inside my own home or my community. As an adult, I evaluated and decided if my environment or experiences growing up were the way I wanted to raise my future children, which helped me decide what kind of life I wanted to provide for them. My daddy issues were front and center and present in my daily living. Each time I looked in the mirror my unknown side would haunt me. I was a mystery to myself and others. All the questions about my skin color and differences drove me insane. If it wasn't for the four-letter word, *love*, I never would have made it.

Love from my family was key to my health. Love from my daddy. Love for myself was another. These were the three certainties that were transparent.

After my parents' separation in 1978, my identity crisis was at its highest. I wished that mirrors didn't exist. In fact, they did more harm than good to my self-esteem because they told me the truth. Mirrors confirmed what those kids at school saw that I couldn't. This harsh truth hit me in my face. I was different. Not inferior, but *different* from the people I loved the most. I was lost, unable to find my way. I was confused. Why did I have to be the *one* who was different? Why did people always have to question my identity? It was a scratched broken record that kept playing, like when my mother and Alfred argued. It would never turn off. I couldn't turn it off or disassociate myself from it. Because it was me all along that had the issue. Mama didn't, and neither did Daddy. They equally loved me and didn't see the difference. I wanted Daddy to see the difference in me, but he never said or did anything to acknowledge it. It was an open secret. An uncovered lie. Or maybe it wasn't a lie? Maybe my dad didn't care about DNA theory. Maybe he never thought long and hard about whether he'd be able to save his daughter Tammy if she needed a blood transfusion or an organ. Or vice versa. I was his daughter based on his heart and soul and he didn't care about the theory. But I cared, and it mattered so much to me growing up, my number one priority was to make sure all my children had the *same* father. My children would not be different. They all would look the same along with their skin complexions. When they looked in the mirror, both sides of them would be equally known. Complete. Fulfilled. It was my mission to have multiple children with *one* father. One love.

When I was with my dad, it was one love. My parents' relationship taught me that their primary focus was my siblings and me. Even though their love for one another fell by the wayside, the love they had for us was unequivocally genuine. My father wanted each of us to have a better life than him. He stressed the importance of school. He was hands on and spent quality time with us. He visited us based on his work schedule, not Mama's or the court system. My daddy was a constant. He and my mother were our protectors.

So when Daddy became ill, we didn't take it too seriously because he downplayed it like it was nothing. His high blood pressure and working in the Texas heat doing construction didn't deter him. He was a hard worker who was an active parent in our lives. And when we received a phone call advising us to rush to the hospital to see my father, we had no idea it would be the final and last time.

My father passed away unexpectedly on September 13, 1985. It was Friday the 13th. A bad luck day according to a lot of superstitious people like Mama and Granddaddy. A day I won't forget. A cruel day. An unjust one. One that I loathed. I was sixteen years old. A recent sixteen-year-old. My birthday was in June. I was only three weeks into my junior year of high school. School had begun, but now I had to do it alone without my biggest cheerleader. The loudest cheer from the crowd had gone silent in the blink of an eye. A light no longer existed inside me and it couldn't be replaced with a new one. No one could replace my daddy, not even my mother if she'd tried. But she never did. She had her role, and my father had his, and he played it well. Just like he played the melodies on the grand piano and sang his unique vocals: "How I wish it would rain." The blue skies didn't go away, and the rain couldn't cover our tears, inside or out. Our bleeding hearts would have to learn to cope with a lifelong loss. We had buried Granddaddy six years before our father, and our grandmother, my dad's mother, was murdered a little over a year before my beloved father passed away.

We had loved and lost a lot in a short span of time. We had lost what was, and what could have been. Our biggest loss was our dad. Our present and future children's grandfather. He had only one grandchild when he died. Argentina was going on four months old, and she lost her grandfather like us, at an early age. Her life was robbed of her grandfather, and so were her siblings and cousins who came later. How unfair and uncertain life can be. Damn you!

That uncertainty reared its ugly head again, as if it hadn't done enough damage. I hated it, and I hated life. I don't know which I despised the most, but I was repulsed by both.

My dad breathed life into me, but he took it away at the same time. He gave me an identity but made me question it. It was like playing spades with the devil in heaven. It had nothing to do with evil, just confusion and conflict. I loved my dad so much. His death traumatized us—meaning his children. I think Mama had washed her hands of Daddy years ago when he left. He left her with a permanent scar, like he did us. Our scar was due to his eternal life's absence, his death. But Mama's was based on betrayal. One that she never got over. And neither did I.

When it was time to make the funeral arrangements, even though she was legally married to Daddy, Mama stayed in the background. She didn't come to the forefront to plan his service. My aunt Debra took care of it. My mother didn't make his current girlfriend, Della, feel insignificant because she was *still* the wife. She didn't want to be known as the wife. And no one who attended my father's funeral could tell. But you could tell that we were his children based on our sobs. We were James Campbell's *four* children. Yeah, me too. And he loved us. There was no doubt in my mind that my daddy loved us, and we loved him. We missed our dad. It was evident in the men we chose and the directions we took after his death. He wouldn't have approved, and I can't help wondering how our decisions could have, would have, been different had our father not left Mama. Or if he had lived longer than forty-one years to see his girls and his son mature into adults.

Chapter Seventeen

It's Too Soon

$\mathcal{M}$y mother was my best friend. We talked about everything and there was nothing off limits when it came to our frequent conversations. I remember one day my mom was eating olives. She would always eat them from their glass container. I'd always ask her for some because I loved them too. We were sitting on the front porch in Wheatley Courts when she told me that, "olives taste just like penises." I chuckled because it caught me off guard. I wasn't sure if she said it so that I would stop eating her olives or not. But we cracked jokes and I did silly things to make her laugh.

We were sitting on the same porch listening to the radio and suddenly the radio station had audio difficulties and the music stopped playing. I stood up from my chair and instantly made a dance routine in response to the music not playing. I placed both hands on my stomach and I pushed in to make my butt go backwards and then pushed my butt forward to make it go back to its starting point. I took my hands to the left side of my hips to make them go to the right side and pushed the right side, until my routine landed in the center where I began. As I did each area of the midsection of my body, I sang, "Where the m-u-s-i-c?" repeatedly. My mom busted out laughing at my theatrics. I enjoyed making my mother smile. Her favorite words were, "Tammy, you're something else."

I couldn't have agreed more, like when she taught me to ride a bike. I was five years old and we lived in the Victoria Courts. I had training wheels on my bike, but I wanted them off. I begged Daddy to take them off because I was ready to ride and go fast. Tina and Edward always had bikes and I had a Big Wheel bike and they would leave me for blocks trying to catch them, but when I turned five, I learned to ride a bike. Daddy took the training wheels off and I never looked back. I rode my bike like the professional, Lance Armstrong.

One day my mother was getting after me for something I did. She was trying to give me a butt whipping. I remember running down the stairs and hopping on my bike as she ran after me. She finally quit running when she couldn't catch me, and I kept looking back at her as I peddled faster and faster. She got tired and gave up. I later returned home, and I suppose she forgot about the whipping or she just laughed it off because it was comical that her five-year-old daughter rode her bike to escape the belt.

I wished we could have escaped the projects like I did Mama's belt. Victoria Courts was the first set of public housing we lived in. We didn't live there for long, but it wasn't where I wanted to be.

There was a Mexican family that lived next door to us, and they had a son named Johnny. Johnny and I played and ate watermelon together. When we were eating watermelon, his mother decided to take a Polaroid picture of us. I was standing next to him in a striped tank top eating a big piece of watermelon with juice running down my tummy, which stuck out. His family always suggested that Johnny and I would get married when we grew up, but that wasn't going to happen. His culture and mine were too different. I was marrying someone that had the same complexion as my father.

I don't know if it was Johnny's parents' van that caught fire one night or our neighbors, but it was a scary sight to see. The van was engulfed with smoke and flames, and everyone moved away and watched the firefighters put out the fire. It was a dark and dusty humid night. We didn't wait around to see them put out the fire but when we woke up the next day, the white van was destroyed.

Summer seemed hotter watching that van in flames, but the silver lining was that it was during the time when Catholic nuns would come to the neighborhood and teach us about clay pottery. We would go to the neighborhood gymnasium to get chocolate milk and sack lunches and that's where we met the nuns. We would be outside with them, newspapers plastered on top of tables with clay, making all types of unknown sculptures. We had fun making pottery, but soon after the fire we moved to Morning View Street and I attended Gates Elementary. We never saw Johnny or his family after that.

Soon after Daddy passed, Mama and I were sitting on the front porch of Wheatley Courts talking. She wanted to tell me about DeWhight so bad that it was like money burning a hole in a kid's pockets. But I didn't want to hear it. My father, the man that I'd known as my dad, was gone. DeWhight was the last person I wanted to talk about. But it was important for her to continuously tell me about someone that I hated. Well, I didn't hate him. I just didn't like him. I *loved* my daddy. And it was too soon after his death to be talking about my biological sperm donor. I'd rolled my eyes and told her that I didn't care about him. He wasn't my daddy. Unfortunately, he was, but I couldn't change that and neither could he. I wanted to, but since I couldn't, my disdain for him was taken out on every boy that came into my life. They were disqualified instantly if they were light skinned. I couldn't marry or date someone who had a strong possibility of being my half-brother. I wished my checkpoints had stopped at skin color, but they didn't. If a man was in the military, that was another "STOP," don't go there. I hated all men in the military. The fine men that were protecting our country. They gave me no reason to dislike them, but my loathing for DeWhight left me no choice. These constant barriers became more relevant in my life as I grew older.

Chapter Eighteen

Older Men Younger Girls

I had just turned seventeen in the summer of 1986. My father's passing had taken its toll on all of us. He was no longer in our lives like he was before. My siblings and I had no father figure, or anyone remotely qualified to take my father's place. My body was changing into a woman's and puberty began to rear its ugly head by attacking my precious *light skinned* face. It seemed like each morning that I rose I had a new zit on my high cheekbones. I had perfect skin until I turned sixteen, but it just kept getting worse, and so did my self-esteem. It had gotten so bad that one day I was walking to the neighborhood Steve's Store when I was approached by a light-skinned man in his mid-twenties. He had a Jheri Curl and a gold tooth. I tried to let him pass before I crossed his path, but he waited for me. I had never seen him before, so we didn't know each other by name or face when he walked up to me. He took his unclean forefinger, stroked it against my cheek, and said, "You know I can take care of all of this, right? Get rid of it all." He emphasized this with a grin that warranted a slap across his face. Not because of his smile, but for putting his hands on me and violating my private space with an insult. I thought to myself, if my daddy was here, right now, he would have kicked his ass. How dare a grown man touch his seventeen-year-old daughter suggesting that sex with him could take away her puberty acne.

This is when I realized how bold and disrespectful men were to women. Except I wasn't a woman, I was a young girl.

An innocent child trapped in an environment that scarred me for life. Men of all ages chased me around the projects like it was dove hunting season. I wasn't a piece of meat, I was me. And I needed my father to protect me from them. It was a fight of the fetish, constantly being whistled at like I was a Labrador retriever fetching a flying Frisbee. It was tiring. And I was tired of running. My track shoes were worn and burned out. My soul-searching to be complete was exhausting. It was like running a marathon with no finish line. There was no end in sight. I looked for similarities in people to try and make me whole. Complete. I wanted to be treated the way my father treated me. He put my sisters and me on pedestals. We had our own individual pedestals because he loved his daughters *equally*. He favored no one. But these men couldn't hold a candle in comparison to my dad. My dad would never chase young girls around or try to get in their panties. He married my mother, a woman, and I had never known him to even look at young teenage girls in any sexual manner. These men disgusted and angered me because they were nothing like my father and they robbed me of my childhood by wanting to do sexual things for adults. I wanted to be held inside warm arms, not cold hearts. Like my father used to do. I wanted to sit on top of laps like I did with my dad. I wanted love and compassion, but in a *fatherly* way. Instead, I got all the wrong things for all the wrong reasons.

When I was growing up, it seemed like a major sport for older men to want young teenage girls. And they would stop at nothing to acquire their prize. My mother tried to shield me the best that she could, but she needed the same protection. She learned the hard lessons. *You must learn to protect yourself by any means necessary.* And she did—her and her children. But the constant almost daily attacks on me were too much to bear. She defended me against ninety percent of men, but the other ten percent were let inside disguised in sheep's clothing. These men were master manipulators, hustlers, jive turkeys, and familiar. One man was so familiar that he waited for me and I unknowingly waited for him. It was the beginning of five years later.

Chapter Nineteen

Dat Smile

𝘐 never understood death until my grandfather passed away. I don't think I knew what was going on, but I could tell that something was different and we wouldn't be seeing him anymore. But it was my father's unexpected death six years later that opened my eyes. It was cruel, unfair, life-changing, abandonment. His death was a tragedy. I often reminisce on what decisions I would have made had my dad been in my life. Would I have joined the Air Force after high school? Would I have been a victim of the Wheatley Courts? I needed my father's constant cheers from the crowd. He kept me pushing forward with his praise. He was inspirational. I didn't want to disappoint him so I gave it my all when he was here.
I didn't talk to anyone about my feelings or how his death affected me. I was lost in an environment that swallowed teenage girls whole. I had no chance or choice.

Living in the Wheatley Courts was the biggest tragedy.

        I'd known him and his smile since I was twelve years old. I watched him when he was a teenager even though he always looked older than his age. He was a football player and maybe that's why he was so big and strong. Big as in a solid muscular build, not overweight. Even though I never asked him if he knew me, something told me that he did by our first conversation.

Garland and I officially met when I turned seventeen years old. When he introduced himself, I cut it short because I'd known him five years before. His sister and I cheered together and played sports. His mother was always at our sporting events. She often had her camera in hand and took many pictures.

G.J. was his nickname and it was short for Garland Jerome. I was the captain of the Emerson Bobcat cheerleaders, so I wasn't sure if he had seen me cheer or playing sports, or if he had seen me in one of the pictures his mother took.
He was observant and paid attention to details, but he never said if he knew me, or knew of me, and I never asked. But his smile on our first meeting spoke like an Inspector Gadget that said he definitely knew or investigated me. And it was one of the reasons we dated. We were *familiar* with each other. We were together off and on for about two years. In that two-year timeframe, he never mentioned his father. His parents were divorced, and he lived with his mother, along with his sister and brother. His brother was one year older than him and his sister was seventeen like me. He was twenty-one.

I knew he was my sister Tina's age because she knew him as well from school.

G.J.'s and my connection was instant. When he'd see me, his eyes and smile would light up like it was Christmas. He truly was smitten over me and the feeling was mutual. I don't know what it was about him that made me want to be caressed and loved. He gave the sincerest hugs and affection. I would melt in his arms when he hugged me. I'd never met anyone who could give hugs like G.J. I was addicted to them.

But since I was a virgin, that's all I wanted to do—sit on his lap while he embraced me. It was fine in the beginning, but that changed because he wanted more than hugs. Me sitting on his lap all the time wasn't good enough. He became impatient because he needed more. I wasn't willing to give more, so we clashed for eight months, going back and forth about sex. His pressuring me was difficult, but I held my ground until he finally left me with a band of gold. He gave me a tri-gold wedding ring before he finally gave up, but he didn't ask me to marry him. He said that he was taking me to Vegas to get married. It was *his* way of saying "let's get married." I was only seventeen and there was no way I was getting married. He left, and it was another abandonment that I had to deal with.

I graduated in 1987, a month after he left. He never mentioned breaking up or why he left. He just did. He was at my commencement to see his sister graduate, but he was with his son's mother. Oh, did I mention that he had a son? He did, and he was crazy about him. The same way he was crazy about his beloved family. He told me about his son when we first met, so it wasn't a secret. He said he was no longer with his son's mother, but he would go and see him, and that was it. I knew when he visited his son because I'd see the car seat in the back of the car, but it was rare that I saw it. And since I was young, I didn't ask questions because I trusted him. It was a huge mistake because he lied about Wendy, his son's mother. He was still with her, as I found out later in our relationship.

G.J. abandoning me was devastating. I loved him. He was my first teenage love, though I don't know why I loved him so much because his raging hormones were stressful. He would treat me bad, then return the next day apologetic, and I'd be right back in his warm embrace. His charm was intoxicating, and I stayed drunk in love. This was our norm. If we weren't fighting about sex, we were at odds about his jealousy and controlling ways. He wanted me all to himself, and I didn't mind because I wanted the same. But he was living a double life. One that consisted of me and his children's mother. Children plural—he had a daughter too. Though it was never clear whether his daughter was conceived before or during the time he and I were dating. Either way, he never mentioned a daughter. She was born after he left me. She was premature, so I could understand why he had to leave and be there for his family. I admire him for supporting his daughter, though I didn't know what was going on at the time. I learned about her birth soon after we reunited in 1988. He still hadn't told me about her. He said he left because he wasn't right for me, that I was a good girl and he didn't want to taint me. But he was back temporarily, and soon after, we began having sex when I was nineteen. I can count on two hands the number of times we had sex. I didn't enjoy it. I did it to satisfy him and I felt obligated. There was nothing wrong on his behalf. I just wasn't ready and felt I was too young. *If* I had been ready, I would have enjoyed it more.

One day I received a phone call from G.J.'s children's mother telling me everything about their relationship. I couldn't believe it. *My G.J.* was cheating and lied. It was another heartbreak. Why I allowed him to break my heart, then put the pieces back together, only to break it again was beyond me. I was a glutton for punishment.

During the time that G.J. abandoned me, I began dating my brother's friend, Darryl. Darryl lived outside of the East Terrace, but his mother lived in the projects. He had a sister named Tammy. He often visited his mother, but he never mentioned his father. There was no man around. Darryl was twenty-one and I was eighteen when we began dating. He would take me around his family, and they would party and drink like him. He was an alcoholic and he couldn't go a day without a forty-ounce beer. It seemed like he could control his alcoholic behavior because he was never violent. It made him smile all the time and relax. I didn't see anything wrong at the time because both my father and grandfather drank, and from what I remembered neither were violent.

There were a lot of unknowns about Darryl that I found out through my brother, and later, after his arrest. His imprisonment gave G.J. the opportunity to reel me back in with his bait and hook. It didn't take much because I still loved him. G.J.'s smile was deadly and I must have died a dozen deaths when I was with him. We were so perfect for each other that we were imperfect. After leaving him over his infidelity and beginning a relationship with his arch-enemy, his rival, things began to really spin out of control for me. I dropped out of college and contemplated joining the Air Force. I had plenty of time to escape G.J.'s pain. I ran far away from him when I discovered his double life.

When talking to Wendy, I discovered her relationship with him was the total opposite of mine. I couldn't believe some of the things she told me about him. I don't see how she stayed, though obviously I could see that she loved him and had kids with him. But when was enough, enough? He had no intention of marrying Wendy. According to her, he never proposed or gave her a ring. She lived in a rough neighborhood known as the New Light Village. It was low-income housing, and better than the Wheatley Courts, but not much better. Wendy lived there with her children and G.J. part-time because I was always out with him, or he was at his mother's house, it was a weird arrangement. One that allowed him to cheat on both Wendy and me, and convinced me that he was single.

Wendy was two years older than me. She attended Sam Houston High School but didn't finish. I have no idea when or how they met, but she worked at Popeye's with Darryl before we started dating.

G.J. picked her up from work and took her money, according to her. I had never known him to work, but he always had money, so he could have been getting it from her. I didn't know his side of the story, but Wendy seemed honest, so I took her to be credible. She let me into private parts of her life, though I didn't ask to be there. I'm glad I had enough decency to listen to her and leave G.J., which many women wouldn't have done. I left because Wendy and G.J. reminded me of my mother and father's relationship, and how Dad cheated on Mom. I always wanted the other women to leave my parent's marriage alone, but they wouldn't. I didn't want to be like any of those mistresses. I deserved my own man, and he found me shortly after I broke it off with G.J. The irony is, I followed in my mother's footsteps, just the way she escaped my father and went with Alfred.

Chapter Twenty

From The Frying Pan into the Fire

I had just gotten off work at Taco Bell and still had on my uniform when I walked inside my home to find my brother anxiously telling my mother that a Mexican guy was planning to kill me because I broke into their home and robbed his father. My sister lived next door to the guy that was looking for me, and my brother had tried to explain to him that I wouldn't do anything like that. But the Mexican guy insisted that it was a girl named Tammy based on reports from his father and witnesses, and I was the only Tammy that he knew. I had no idea what he was talking about since I had just gotten off work.

I robbed an old man? I robbed his father and he was going to kill me! What? I'd heard a lot of things in my life, but this was by far the most ridiculous and outlandish bullshit ever. I was scared. *Someone was trying to kill me for something I didn't do, and I had just walked past his house?*

My mother, who never left home without her gun, went to retrieve it, and she, my brother, and I walked together looking for the guy trying to kill me. My mom was going to kill him before he got to me over something I didn't do.

As we turned the corner to get to the guy's house, we saw a police car. The guy looking for me was outside his father's home talking to a cop named Red. Red knew everyone from the neighborhood. Back in the days when the police were driving through the hood, the code name to alert everyone of their presence was *rollers*.

90

One day the policemen were driving through the hood with their megaphone in hand, and they were laughing and joking saying, "rollers." They had caught on to the code name and were no longer fooled by hood slang.

Red was one of the policemen that often frequented the Wheatley Courts and joked around with the residents. He knew where to find anyone he was looking for. I'm sure there were a few snitches helping him. But when we walked over to Red's patrol car to see what was going on, Red pointed to me and said, "This is Tammy Campbell. She works at Taco Bell. She wasn't the one that broke into your father's house."

I was shocked when Red said that. I didn't know he knew so much about me. Red went on to explain that there were two Tammy's, but that the other Tammy had a criminal history of burglary and robbery. The Tammy they wanted was Darryl's sister, Tammy. I was glad the situation was handled, but even though the guy apologized for the mistaken identity, my mom didn't accept his apology. She didn't take kindly to someone looking to kill *her* Tammy. You didn't mess with Bobby Jean's kids, especially me. My mother didn't play, and she meant business when she went looking for the guy. He had an Uzi, but my mother had her .38 Smith & Wesson, and it was good enough for her. She was going to kill him before he killed me. This was our life in the Wheatley Courts. Even if you didn't look for trouble it would find you.

Trouble came looking and found me because he saw me at Taco Bell. He saw me before he went to jail and when he got out, and he saw me working when he applied for a job. I didn't see him that day because he said I was busy and didn't notice him, but the truth was, I only had eyes for G.J.

He wanted a job but he was trying to get next to me too. It was his priority and I still don't know which was more important, me or the job. He didn't get the job because I had a manager that was an asshole. He and I couldn't get along because I was a shift manager and he was the manager, but I ran the store better than him. He couldn't understand how a nineteen-year-old could do that, or how I got the employees to listen to me but he couldn't get them to work. I got them to listen and work because I treated them with respect, like they were human. I had a saying that if you kept the customers happy and the store clean, then you could sit down and do whatever you wanted. If the employees' families came to Taco Bell, I would allow them to give their families food at no cost. Instead of paying fifty percent for their employee meals, I allowed them to eat free. They enjoyed working with me, *not* for me. We were a team and that's how I wanted it to be. I considered my employees my business partners. We took care of the customers and each other. I was young and inexperienced, but I was good at what I did. I trusted my employees and they trusted me.

I was a gullible teenager and was taken advantage of by many. Before I bought my first car, I caught the bus to work. I was supposed to be off this day, but I was called in to help because an employee was ill. The bus was crowded and I scooted over so this young Black girl could sit next to me. She was very pretty and reminded me of Thelma from the TV series *Good Times*. Across from us I noticed two Black men playing a board game where they had to pick where a ball was hidden under a bottle cap. I didn't pay them much attention until the young black girl came to sit right next to me. She sat down and immediately began playing the game with the two men. I peeped at what was going on but still didn't want to be involved since I didn't know her or the men. She was pulling out twenty-dollar bills and was jumping in her seat from excitement. This went on for about five minutes. After playing about three rounds of "find the ball," she looked at me and asked if I wanted to play. I told her "no." She said, "come on, it's easy." She began playing again and winning. She nudged me on my shoulder and kept telling me to try it. I looked at her beautiful face and thought about how much money she had won. I reluctantly agreed because she wouldn't take no for an answer. I opened my wallet and pulled out a twenty-dollar bill. I was told to find the ball. I chose a top, but to my dismay, when the guy uncovered the cap, there was no ball. I was shocked because I saw the ball under that cap. She persuaded me to try again and win my money back, but I only lost again. Fortunately, it was my bus stop and I exited. I felt like a fool, having lost my forty dollars in a matter of minutes playing a stupid game. The patrons on the bus looked at me as I tried to disguise my disappointment. But their stares said it all: "You big dummy!"

I walked to the nearest pay phone to call my mother. As I dialed to tell Mama what had happened, I saw the two guys and girl exit the bus together at the next stop, and that's when I knew I had been conned out of my money. I was devastated. I cried while telling my mother everything. I called my job and told them that I couldn't come in after all. I caught the bus back home and my mother and I went to the bus stop where the guys first got on, hoping to catch them there. But no such luck. Unfortunately, this was the story of my life as a gullible teenager. And shortly after this incident is when I went from the frying pan into the fire when I met *trouble*, Bobby.

Chapter Twenty-One

Dear Mr. Mailman

I've always had male friends that I would chill with when I was between boyfriends, and at times, I would go by their jobs when I needed something. I had a friend named Lonnie who worked at Church's Chicken on New Braunfels Street, and whenever I was hungry and wanted chicken, I'd go by his job to get free chicken. I'd always promised to let him take me out on a date, but I never obliged.

I met a mailman one day while he was delivering mail. He saw me and we immediately exchanged phone numbers. He lived a few blocks from Wheatley Courts near G.J.'s mother's house on E. Houston. It was a small, nice, quiet, cozy home. He kept it very clean. When I'd get off work at Taco Bell, I'd go by his house to pick up a plate of food. He'd cook me whatever I requested. I often requested enchiladas, and he was a pretty good cook. He did whatever I asked of him. He was about thirteen years older than me, and being nineteen, I took his kindness for weakness.

I wanted to go to the movies to see *School Daze*. I also wanted the cassette tape, *Atlantic Starr*, and asked if we could stop by the music store and get it before going to the movies. He agreed. We stopped to pick up the cassette tape and went inside Windsor Park Mall to the theater. We walked in and it wasn't too crowded, which I was glad about because I was still seeing G.J during this time. I didn't want him or any of his cousins to see me.

He bought me popcorn, soda, and nachos.

We took our seats toward the back in the center of the theatre.

He didn't want any snacks, though I offered him some. The movie began and he was laughing a lot throughout. I didn't think it was *that* funny. In fact, I was bored. I got my cassette tape and was ready to leave.

While I sat there bored out of my mind. He continued to laugh. I asked him what was so funny, and he turned to me in his accented monotone voice and said, "Give me a break."

I looked at him and said, "What?"

He repeated, "Give me a break."

The little smart mouth teenager that I was looked at him in a repulsed manner and said, "Excuse me, I don't drink after nobody."

He looked at me and said, "Huh?"

I rolled my eyes and repeated, "I don't drink after nobody." Then I pulled my soda from the cup holder and drank from my straw.

"What are you talking about? I said, *give me a break.*"

I felt dumb. I thought he said, "*Give me a drink.*" I didn't even apologize. I got up from my chair and told him that I had to go to the restroom. I did go, but on my way back I saw *Ms. PacMan*, a video game machine. I stopped and played a few games and then I played *Galaga*. I was taking my sweet time because I didn't want to be there with Mr. Mailman. I was using him. It hurts me to type this about myself, but I was young and he was so nice and sweet. Looking back, he would have made a great husband, but for a woman his own age. He had hair on his chest and that grossed me out for some odd reason. Everything about him made me clam up. After the movie date, I came by his home one more time to get a plate of enchiladas that I took to G.J. and I told him that I had cooked it.

I didn't see him anymore after that. He was too old and too good for me. I was a young teenybopper still in love with G.J. I regret how I treated Mr. Mailman and I often think about him and hope to see him one day so I can apologize for the way I treated him. He didn't deserve it.

If he ever reads this book, I want him to know how young and confused I was at that time. I appreciated everything he did for me and I'm sorry it didn't work out between us. It wasn't him; it was me. I truly hope that he found someone to treat him like a king.

Dear Mr. Mailman,
I'm sorry from the bottom of my heart.
Please forgive me for my immature ways.
I didn't intend to leave without a word to say.
I wanted to stay but I couldn't because my heart
belonged to someone else from the start.
I didn't mean to do what I did, and I hope that you could
forgive me and that you found a better mate.
I will always remember you as a good man and the one
that I foolishly threw away.

Chapter Twenty-Two

Karma

I should have run him over when he jumped in front of my car as I pulled into the parking space in front of my mama's house. It had been a long day at work and it was dark, so I had an excuse if I had hit him. I mean, who jumps in front of a car? Don't answer that—I'll tell you. It was Bobby. One of the notorious playboys in the Wheatley Courts. I knew of him, but didn't really know him. He needed to be known and it was his duty to get to know me.

He needed no introduction since we had met years before he went to prison. He was drawn back to me like he hadn't been gone for two years, and one of his first questions was if I was still with G.J. He had done his research on me. I was no longer with G.J since I had learned he was cheating on me. I made my status known: I was *single* and nineteen. He made a mental note, and that meant a green light to go and don't slow down.

Bobby and I were inseparable. He made me his woman instantly without confirming it with me. He confirmed it with himself and I accepted it for what it was. After he introduced himself to my mother, we began hanging out all during the wee hours of the night. I was intrigued by his demeanor. He was born in San Antonio, Texas but when he was eighteen he was sent to Dallas to live with his mother. He was in and out of foster care as a child and ran away from those foster homes. Shortly before I met him, he was a nomad. His mother lived in

Dallas with her boyfriend who abused her. Bobby jumped into one of their fights and she got mad at him and sent him back to live with his beloved grandmother in San Antonio. He never got along with his mom. She had him when she was fifteen years old and his father was never around either. We'd go visit his father at the gym or YMCA where he worked. Every time he'd bring me around, his father would mention my complexion. Bobby and his father loved light-skinned women. It was their preference. His father would say that dark-skinned women were mean and evil. I don't know why I didn't correct him at the time. I didn't really know what to say. My sisters and mom were dark skinned and none of them were mean or evil. I didn't understand colorism during that time.

Bobby's upbringing was toxic and the anger and demons he fought daily contributed to how he treated his mother and me. He often made her feel guilty about how she left him to the wolves. He made her cry every chance he got. They couldn't be around each other for long, even though they loved each other. She tried to make amends and be a better mother, but it was a little too late. He was already grown and part of the street life. He was a thug. Trying to be the mother of a thug the age of twenty-six was too late.

When Bobby was around his father, I never heard him say he wasn't in his life as a child. Their conversations were totally different than the ones he had with his mother. He never held his father accountable for his abandonment the way he did his mom. His father had different children from different women. Bobby was the only child by his father on his mother's side of the family. He had four sisters and he was the oldest and only son. He had uncles the same age as him. One of his uncles used to date my sister's friend and he would beat her until she was black and blue.

One day when we were over at Bobby's grandmother's home, his uncle's girlfriend said she didn't want to watch a porn movie with Bobby's grandmother. His grandmother got upset and said that the girl thought she was too good to watch porn with them. I didn't want to watch it either. It made me feel very uncomfortable, so Bobby called me outside and we left. We came back to give his uncle and his girlfriend a ride home. He was upset at her about something, yelling at the top of his lungs while I drove them home. I could imagine what was going to happen to her as soon as they got home. He was a woman beater like Bobby. All of Bobby's uncles were disrespectful to women.

Bobby's great-uncle had a girlfriend with two daughters. We would go to his house and see him belittle and call her a bitch and a hoe in front of everyone. He would talk to her like a dog and she would stand there and take it. He would send her to steal clothes from department stores and sell them on the black market. He was an alcoholic and he was terrible. I often asked her why she was with him, but she didn't know. Just like me. We were all with men who abused us and we stayed. Some of the women were abused severely, but not me. What Bobby did to me was nothing compared to the abuse of his uncles' girlfriends. I fought back, but instead of fighting back, I should have left.

I should have known better when we went with his grandmother and uncle shopping one day. While they were in the store, Bobby got in the front seat of the car and began driving around and around in a circle in the parking lot. He was practicing driving with me in the car. He was twenty-six years old with no driver's license. Even I had my license at eighteen. He parked the car before his uncle and grandmother caught him. He always did spontaneous and criminal acts when we were together.

In the beginning, it excited me, but as I grew older I began to get tired of the street life. Especially after finding out that I was going to have a child. My life was in a tailspin but it was just the beginning.

Chapter Twenty-Three

The Key to my Heart

In 1990, my mom was going through a huge life change that affected all of us. She was the anchor to our ship. She was the head of the estate. She was our backbone. She was the strong protector and unbreakable supermom. To see your mother go from strong to mental illness overnight is devastating. We didn't know anything about paranoid schizophrenic hallucinations, depression, and anxiety. Let me rephrase this—I knew about those conditions in the elderly because I had just graduated from my medication aide class and worked as a Medication Aide at the time my mother was showing signs of mental illness. I never thought that it could or would happen to *my mother*. My mom was hearing voices in her head telling her to kill herself. She was hallucinating that this particular guy who worked at the flea market wanted a romantic relationship with her. She imagined this girl, Theresa, who I'd had a fight with, leading a parade.

The signs of mental illness began to rear their ugly heads when I was nineteen years old in 1989. My mother and I used to have deep intelligent conversations about life, and her life growing up, but our conversations began to change. She began talking "crazy" as many people would describe it. It wasn't crazy to me, but it was uncharacteristic. I began to question the medicine she was taking. She was prescribed valium and many other psychotropic drugs. She frequented the community health center on Commerce Street for psychiatric therapy. But something wasn't right, and I didn't know what it was at the time. She would get better in spurts, so she would go back to being her "normal" self but then the hallucinations, massive headaches, and paranoia would return with a vengeance. She was taken by police force the first time to the State Hospital on South Presa Street.

I will never forget the night they took my mother in for psychiatric evaluation. I was told she was aggressive and fighting with the police. I had just gotten off work at Taco Bell and I didn't see the beginning of the incident that took place, but my mother's family, my brother, and sisters were there for my mom. We all followed in separate cars, the police car to see where they were taking my mother. They arrived at a place I didn't recognize, an asylum, before admitting her. I talked to the authorities and they were asking all types of personal questions about my mother. I was brought in to answer a lot of them because I knew the most about our mother. I knew her social security number. I always photographed important information inside my memory.

I wanted to see my mother, but they wouldn't let us. We had to see her the next day. We visited her many days after the initial entry into the asylum until she was released. She was in and out of the state hospital for about two years. She loathed each visit. We didn't know anything about mental illness, especially not how or why it was happening to her. It was devastating to say the least.

My mother's mental illness and my pregnancy was way too much to bear. I was with her at the state hospital when my water broke. I thought I was peeing on myself, but it was my mom who told me what was happening. Fortunately, I was with Tina. My mom wasn't allowed to leave, although she wanted to be with me. She was not in a frame of mind to do so. She hadn't come back to her "normal" self and it was taking longer to do so than previous times. I wanted my mom back.

Tina and I left to go to the hospital, and eleven hours later, I had Myson. I phoned my mother so she wouldn't worry and let her know that we were both okay. I was released from the hospital the day after having my son, and my mother was released from the asylum on July 02, 1992. She was finally able to hold her grandson. She looked at him and said that he had my lips but looked like Bobby. She loved my son and wanted to take care of him, but she couldn't. Her mental illness had taken its toll. I knew it but didn't tell her. It was written all over her face. She had a lot of strange behaviors, like her affinity for the lotto tickets that had just come to the state of Texas. I would go buy her lotto tickets and she would scratch them off. The minute she didn't win, she wanted to go back to the store immediately and buy more. We'd go buy more and the minute she'd lose, she wanted you to go back to the store to get her more. It was harmless and repetitive but bizarre behavior from my mom. Nevertheless, it took a lot of patience to deal with. She often sent Terrie or me to get her lotto tickets.

Terrie had thrown a barbecue for the Fourth of July. My mom was only on a two-day furlough before she had to return to the state hospital, so she wasn't able to attend the festivities. Her visits were constant for the next four months. I'd go visit her often when I wasn't working, but she wasn't getting better. In fact, she seemed more depressed because she hated the hospital. She wanted to be at home. The doctors had my mother on so many medications and now that I look back, the side effects of those medications made her worse. We didn't know what to do for her.

My mother's illness, along with raising my son alone, was draining the life out of me. I was going through postpartum blues. My sister's phone call on August 28, 1992 took me over the edge as well. She called and told me that G.J had been found dead on the front lawn of a home and that it was on the news. I couldn't believe it because I had just seen him a few weeks prior to his death. Even though he and I were no longer together, and I often ran into him throughout the years, his death still hurt. He was my first love and now he was gone. A senseless crime had robbed him of his life at twenty-seven years old. I felt bad for his children and his children's mother. I knew and understood their pain. *My* Garland Jerome Woods, that smile, I would never see again. But his memory will live on and I will make certain that he's never forgotten. Rest in peace, G.J.

You will always have a key to my heart.

Chapter Twenty-Four

Shero

It didn't take long for Bobby to return to jail after G.J's death and our son's birth. It was his home away from home. Sometimes I'd think he was homesick if he wasn't constantly in jail. I waited for him to get his life together, but he never did. Although he tried, the demons he fought overcame any progress he tried to make. He was damaged from the time he was in and out of those foster homes. His family was the same, all damaged and fighting their own demons. They drank like sailors. They were toxic and draining to be around. My man fighting demons and my mother's mental illness were the center of my life along with my son and work. Balancing all four was no easy task and I wouldn't wish it on anyone, including my enemies.

The only true enemy I had was the one with a stronghold on my beloved mother. I resented and loathed everything she was going through. She had a fight with one of the residents at the state hospital and someone tried to rape her as well. She was furloughed the day after the rape attempt. She came home and never returned to the place that she hated most.

On November 07, 1992, my mother endured her last and final fight with those demons when she leaped to her death from the Walters Street Bridge. Tina phoned me to deliver the bad news and my world turned upside down in a matter of seconds. Mama was dead. My beloved mother, whom I had loved with all my heart for twenty-three years. First Daddy was dead and now my mother. I cried like an infant. My cries turned to anger at the Lord. I wanted to do what the Jews had done to Jesus and kill him again for taking my mother away from me when I needed her most. But my mother had already died when mental illness took over in 1990, and it was a slow, cruel death. She was never the same person.

On November 11th, my mother's physical body was laid to rest. Mama was gone. Her disdain for the asylum along with poverty had killed her. She'd opted for death rather than return to either one. Many will say that Mama took the *easy* way out, but have you ever tried to kill yourself and succeeded? My mother was a fighter, a warrior, a soldier. She fought twenty-four seven for forty-six years. She was tired and felt that she had already raised her children. She often repeated this when she was alive. She was beyond tired of the poverty, headaches, and the ghettos. All three killed my mother. My Mama was and will always be my strength, my best friend, and my Shero.

Chapter Twenty-Five

My Sonshine

Mama was exhausted. She had raised her four children, and often said she felt that we no longer needed her. But it was difficult to know if it was her speaking, or the mental illness. Mental illness is shunned or never talked about in the Black community. We are taught to keep our personal lives private and not go telling any personal business. Therapy or psychiatrists are for "crazy" people. You are seen as weak if you can't solve your own problems.

Poverty is rampant. Our history is whitewashed, distorted, destroyed, and hidden. Black people are treated like third-class citizens in their own country. Our main health diagnoses are high blood pressure, stroke, and diabetes. Many will blame our health issues on things like no health insurance, bad diets, or self-destruction. The diagnosis of mental illness is overlooked and underdiagnosed. Untreated mental illness is abundant. We need to shine a light on it, and it needs to happen before it's too late. It was too late for Mama, but it's never too late to share her story, or my family's. Mental illness is a cruel disease. It attacks the mind without warning. It takes control of your, body and soul. Mama had died long before that November the seventh, and I came to the realization that I would be coping with a lifetime of pain. Ever since her death, I have been in the same boat as Bobby, his family, and my mother. I will forever be fighting demons. Sometimes they get the best of me, but I have stayed strong. I'm here today writing my story because of my son. Bobby Jr. is his name, but he's known as Myson (My son). I wrote a poem for him, and ever since he read that poem as a teenager, he has been Myson to his friends. But he is, and will always be, *my* son.

I raised Myson alone for most of his infant, toddler, and kindergarten years. It was mainly the two of us. Bobby was always either in jail, or he and I would argue so he was out of the home. Myson never saw a stable, loving relationship between his father and me. I have pictures of the good times, but they were few and far between. Bobby's family adored Myson after Bobby Sr. took his birth certificate without my knowledge to show his grandmother that his name was on it and Myson was indeed his son.

Myson was born light skinned like me, and since his father was dark skinned, the family wondered why or how our son came out so "light." Bobby tried to explain that since I was light skinned that was the reason his son was light skinned too. I was appalled that they had questions about the paternity of my child. My response was, "I would have blamed the daddy on a rich man, not a poor one." The audacity of them to question, "Who was the father?" But the birth certificate he showed them seemed to have assuaged their doubts because from that day forward it was "Lil Bobby," a name that close family and friends called our son to distinguish him from his father.

Myson didn't grow up in poverty the way I did. I worked two and three times as hard to provide him with a better life than I had. He had the best of everything I could give him. What I couldn't provide to Myson was time. I worked so hard to provide for us by working two jobs and going to school full time that I couldn't give him the time that was needed. But when I wasn't working or at school, Myson and I were at the swimming pool, playground, or making home videos. Any type of amusement I could find to show him love and appreciation.

I taught him to swim with him lying on my back. By the time he was five years old, he could swim like a fish. He would dive into six feet of water while doing back flips. I was afraid at first, but he seemed to master it so well I enjoyed every back flip that he did. Myson was a daredevil. He learned things fast. He was an extrovert like his father and needed to be around other children. He was a generous, loving child. He would give me kisses every five minutes, running into the house from wherever he was playing outside. He loved his mother. He often brought me gifts home from school. One day his father asked him why he always brought *me* something but not him. So one morning when Myson was getting ready for kindergarten, he reached inside his backpack, pulled out a sample size tube of toothpaste, and said, "Here you go, Daddy." I laughed loud and hard and said, "Oh, he's saying you need to brush your teeth because your breath stinks." It was so funny, but that's how Myson was. He always brought me gifts and would pick small flowers from outside to bring to me. He was also very anal. When he went to the bathroom in kindergarten, if he didn't wipe his behind good, he would leave streaks in his underwear. He'd phone me from the nurse's office saying that he boo-booed on himself. I'd have to come from work and go to the house to get him clean underwear because he wasn't going to have a good day if I didn't. When I got to his school and gave him the underwear, I'd look at his old pair and realize he hadn't boo-booed on himself, he just had "streaks" from not wiping good. It didn't matter; he didn't want the underwear on his behind. After he called a few more times to bring him clean underwear, I got smart and began putting extra underwear in his backpack so that I wouldn't have to come from work anymore. He was adamant about always having clean underwear.

When Myson's father was home and not in prison, he'd spend quality time with him as well. He often took him to the park, the zoo, or swimming. But the bonding between him and his father never took place because of the inconsistent years when Bobby was gone. Shortly after Myson turned five years old, I left his father and decided to turn my life around. I did a complete one hundred eighty degree turnaround. I took control of my life and stopped doing things that didn't benefit my son and me. I became a loner, putting all my energy into us, and poured all my love into Myson. Nobody came before him, and no one was ever placed in front of him. He was my Sonshine, my only Sonshine, who made me happy when those blue skies were grey. I took him everywhere I went if I wasn't at work or school. I was a hands-on mother. A good young mother. And when I finally left his father, it was Sonshine and I against the world. He was my strength and gave me a reason to live after Mama's death.

Chapter Twenty-Six

On a Mission

I was fortunate enough to meet a guy named Raphael who helped me on my mission. Raphael was Nigerian and his father was not active in his life. He was raised in Nigeria by relatives when his parents came to America for their education. His parents would send money home to his relatives in Nigeria to pay for Raphael and his siblings' schooling. When Raphael and his siblings came of age, they came to America.

Raphael spoke highly of his father. He held a PhD and his mother was an RN. His father was a professor at a university in Dallas, Texas and his mother owned her own senior daycare center for the elderly. His parents divorced shortly after their last daughter was born, though Raphael's mother didn't want a divorce because she loved his father dearly.

Raphael and his father weren't close. It appeared that he had to "prove" to his father that he could become successful like him, but only by making double the money he made. Raphael's mission was to live the American Dream and prove his worth to his father, and with blood, sweat, and tears, he accomplished his goal. In 2010, Raphael graduated with his PhD in pharmacy from the University of Incarnate Word. He married his African Queen and they have four children. Unfortunately, Raphael's father didn't get to see him graduate because he was murdered in 2007 when he went back to visit Nigeria. He was shot and killed. Raphael called me at work to tell me the news about his dad. Although his father didn't see him physically walk the stage and graduate, I'm sure he's somewhere in the universe proudly cheering his son on.

I believe in destiny, and in 1996, Raphael came into my life at the right time and place. He was in school and his ambition to succeed was undeniable. I became amazed at his determination because I too wanted a better life. For years I'd wanted to go back to school but didn't know how I could do it as a single parent. It was Raphael who showed me that I could work double shifts on the weekends and then go to school during the week. He knew about this schedule because his ex-girlfriend was doing it while acquiring her nursing degree. I thought long and hard about it, and the fact that Raphael and his ex-girlfriend were attending school made me envious. But the straw that broke the camel's back was when a nurse at work belittled me. I didn't like it. I knew I was much more than what she thought of me. After the belittling incident I began making plans, and ten years after quitting school I made the decision to return. I was on a mission—nothing and no one was going to get in my way. I heard the silent cheers of my father, pushing me. He wanted me to become an RN, but after working in long-term care, I knew I couldn't stand the sight of blood and ulcers or sores that would always form on residents. I never liked to clean dead bodies either. This wasn't the career field for me.

It was a nurse at my job who suggested that I go into the computer field. I didn't know much about computers in 1996. I didn't even own one. But her suggestion is what I decided to go with, so I sought more information. I spoke with a counselor at San Antonio College and made an appointment to discuss attending school. I learned that I needed to clear my defaulted student loan before I was able to register. I cleared my loan debt and registered in the fall of 1997.

I was twenty-eight when I returned to school. I felt old going to class with eighteen year olds and students who had just graduated high school. But I didn't let my age deter me. I thought back to when I attended college at eighteen and how poverty and my environment determined my fate. I was no longer living in the ghetto, but I was a single mom and responsible for my son's life.

It was scary and I faced many challenges. I cried many days and nights. I would work until sunup and sundown and still study. I brought the work on myself, so I had to sleep in the bed that I made, but I did, and I did it well. I was an honor roll student and earned many scholarships. I saved all my money from the scholarships to take care of my son and me. Every penny that I acquired, I saved. When I got my income tax refund, I saved it. I bought used textbooks for my classes and would only buy new when I couldn't find used.

I never bought many clothes for myself, but I bought my son the best clothes and shoes. He had every Michael Jordan Air Jordan that came out when he was young. I never wanted him to feel the slightest notion that we were poor. We lived like we were middle class because of my money management skills. When rent was due on the first of the month it was paid on the first of the month. Any credit card debt was paid on time, and I paid it off frequently.

My FICO credit score was well into the 700s after I called and had the defaulted student loan removed from my credit report. I knew how important it was to maintain good credit. Credit was at times better than cash. I lived below my means. I was so frugal that by the time I graduated, I had no student loan debt. I didn't owe the government a penny and that in itself was a success. School was a business and my degree was in Business Information Systems. I took life seriously and was on a mission to become successful.

Chapter Twenty-Seven

Obsessed

I looked into the mirror daily and wondered: *who am I?* Where did I acquire my ambition and determination? I was a go-getter and failure was never an option. But the enigma began to enter my thoughts after Mama had passed away. I wanted to know about my biological father. It didn't seem to matter when I was younger because I knew who my dad was. But the older I became, the more the mystery of my unknown father began to rear its ugly head. I talked to Raphael about finding my biological father.

It was 1998, computers were coming of age, and the internet was available. Raphael came to my house one day with a yellow floppy disk in his hand. Once we put it into the hard drive of the computer that floppy disk contained names and phone numbers of different Dwhight Wilsons from the Denver, Colorado area. Raphael wanted me to call each one to see if I could find my father. I was scared, wondering what I could say to a man I didn't know who didn't know me. Besides, these were long distance calls and I didn't want to charge them on my phone bill. Raphael took it upon himself to call the phone numbers asking questions. His Nigerian dialect made calling these strangers even more challenging. I didn't want to call anymore because we weren't getting anywhere, and I didn't know how much my long-distance charges would be until I received the bill a month later. It was almost four-hundred dollars. I was shocked and angry at Raphael because that was one of my concerns about calling long distance. I let

Raphael know what he had done, and he paid the charges on my bill. After the bill was paid, I made a few calls and talked with someone who told me that people had called him before seeking Dwight Wilson but there were two from the Denver, Colorado area. He wasn't the one I was looking for. My search had come to a dead end.

But the more people questioned my ethnicity the more curious I became. I would get furious with strangers wanting to know because I had no answers. It reminded me of those kids in elementary school who always questioned my identity by asking, "Why don't you look like your brother?"

I began to regret not listening when Mama tried to talk to me about DeWhight and I hadn't wanted to hear it. Now, at twenty-eight years old, I was mature enough to hear what she wanted to tell me. Mama had all the answers but was no longer available. It drove me insane. I wanted to know my medical history as well. I hated every question I was asked about my *biological* father. I was confused, and at times I gave my dad's history, not remembering the blood that ran through his veins wasn't the same as mine. I wouldn't change it when I did remember. I left it as-is to avoid questions I didn't have the answers to.

In my mind and heart, my biological father was the man who raised me until his death. This was a comforting lie so I wouldn't have to deal with the harsh reality.

There were days I resented Mama, but then I loved her too much. I always wondered *why me?* Why did I have to be different? Paying for your parents' "mistakes" was unfair and cruel, but there was nothing I could do about it, and the fact that I had no control over it made me obsessed with finding the answers. I thought about DeWhight more often than not. Society never let me forget him.

I was at a nightclub with some coworkers from my job and we were doing Karaoke. After we finished singing *It's Raining Men*, a Mexican guy walked up to me, intrigued. I don't think our performance was that good, but he thought I was beautiful. He offered to buy me a drink and I told him not without buying my friends one, too. He bought my friends drinks and they high-fived me for it. Unfortunately, accepting drinks from a man is the wrong thing to do because afterward they feel they have the right to your attention the entire night. I didn't want to be rude, so I continued to let him bore me to death. He was a good-looking guy, but during this time I was already dating a guy named Walter and I was going to his condo after the club. I looked very sexy with a silky baby blue blouse and striped baby blue mini skirt. I worked out religiously and you couldn't pinch an inch of fat on my abs. It was all going well until we were leaving the club and the guy walked me outside. He wanted to know if he could see me again, but before he asked for my telephone number, he asked if I was Puerto Rican. I laughed and said no, I'm Black. The laughter was a cover to hide my anger.

He, like many, was curious about my ethnicity. Usually people would ask if I was from Louisiana. Even when Raphael and I took a trip to Louisiana, people would ask where I was from. I would say "Texas." I wondered why people always asked if I was from Louisiana and thought to myself, *are there a lot of light-skinned people in Louisiana?* It wasn't until years later that I understood why they asked—it was because of the Creoles. I relaxed my hair during that time and wore a fake curly ponytail, and not wearing my natural hair made people curious. Their questions about my ethnicity made me livid, and even more curious and confused. I became obsessed with wanting to know who DeWhight was and how he looked. What interests did he have? I watched all light-skinned older gentlemen that were around my mother's age. I stayed away from light-skinned men my age that could potentially be my half-brother. I got details on the families of the men I dated and where they were from. I couldn't imagine unknowingly being in a relationship with a half-brother or distant relative. I didn't date men in the military until Walter years later, because I saw them as players. I eliminated everything that DeWhight was and could have been. I had to have the social security numbers of every man I dated or became closely interested in. If I thought they wouldn't give them to me, I'd sneak and read important mail or look inside their wallets to get the information I needed. I had to have all details of their identity in case I needed them for "child support" if the condom accidentally broke. I needed that assurance in case they skipped town and I couldn't locate them. My mother gave me specific details about DeWhight but it wasn't enough during that time to locate him. I didn't want to be put into that situation. I covered my butt. Each year from 1998 on, I searched for DeWhight but had no luck locating him or his family. I envisioned how I would die without finding him and this was a reality I never wanted to face.

Chapter Twenty-Eight

Smuvblkslk

*7*he men I chose had a lot to do with DeWhight. I may have missed out on some really nice, sweet men because they fell into the "do not date" category. But the men I chose never questioned my identity or ethnicity. Bobby was the only colorist of the bunch. The others never brought up skin complexion. I chose the darkest men that held my interest. I met a few at school, or during the time I was in school. I sought intelligent men, ones that could write a decent love letter or had above-average grammar.

I became a different person when I returned to school. I didn't take mess or tolerate it from anyone and that included my professors.

One day in my civil rights class, I challenged my professor on a lecture she gave about Hitler and she didn't like it. From that day forward she became a public enemy. She graded me low on every essay I turned in. The only reason I passed the class was because she had multiple choice questions too and there was no way she could take those points away unless the answer was wrong. My final grade was 74.4, and according to her grading scale, a 74.5 was needed to get a "B" in the class. I went to her at the end of the semester to ask for the .1 to acquire a "B" because I had to maintain good grades for my scholarships but she said, "no." I went to the dean of her department and brought in my paperwork to show how she graded me low on all of my assignments, but he refused to do anything about it. The grade was final. I took my "C," but I always considered her a racist. I remember the day I challenged her, students in the classroom had warned me that I was in for a long semester because she didn't like being questioned on her lectures. In fact, it was my white friend Tiffany who recommended her to me because she had taken her class the previous semester and made an *easy* "A." When I told Tiffany what happened with my grade, she couldn't believe it. I showed her my papers as well because it shocked me that the dean agreed with the professor.

But the professors never stopped me from going to the deans. I had gone to the dean of another department regarding my statistics class. By the end of the semester, there were only five students left in the class. Everyone had dropped but me, and like a fool I continued to stay because I didn't believe in dropping classes. It was a class that Tiffany and I started together, but she had dropped soon after the semester began. She said the professor graded too harshly and she wouldn't pass. I stayed the entire semester along with four other students. When our grades came in, there were four students who made "Fs" and the other student made a "D." I was livid. I was the student who made the "D." I went storming to the dean's office to report the professor, and again I was shut down and nothing was done.

I continued to advocate for myself and challenged my computer programming professor on a "C" that I made in his class. My final grade was a 78. The semester had ended, and I sent him an email requesting a meeting to discuss my final exam and grade. He accepted my request, and when we met I challenged him on a few questions and told him that each of them were subjective. At the time, he disagreed with me. I explained how I needed to maintain good grades because of my scholarships but he still agreed with the outcome of my grade. I left his office defeated, but when I got home and checked my email, he had sent a message letting me know that he reconsidered what I said and he would change my grade. I received a "B," but not only did I get a grade change, I had finally *won*. A victory for a Black woman in America was hard to come by in a racist school system. It seemed like my entire life had been a fight.

My first fight among many was growing up in poverty. After that, discovering the truth about my real father; living in the ghettos of San Antonio; losing my father and getting involved with no-good men and then losing my beloved mother; raising my son alone and working two jobs while going to school. And last but not least, Walter dumped me for another woman who made more money than me.

I was missing my mother, my best friend. My grades were good, but I was depressed. I didn't see myself growing old. I wanted to raise my son until he was eighteen and then end it like my mother. I didn't want to kill myself, but I was worn out and *tired* from the struggle of life. I wanted and needed relief fast. I wrote poems about life and that kept me sane. My love for my son is what kept me strong and pushed me forward. I adored him and I couldn't have made it without him. He was my heart, soul, breath, and life. He was my Sonshine. We had an unbreakable bond. Nobody came before my son, and the men that I dated had to know where they stood in my life if they ever got involved with me.

I made this transparent, and when I met Mr. Smuvblkslk, aka Nino, in the summer of 2000, he accepted and wanted the full package that included Myson and me. Mr. Smuvblkslk and I met on AOL (America Online). It was an internet service where you could visit and meet people all around the world. Emilio was his given name and Nino was a nickname. His profile name was Smuvblkslk. Emilio and I became a couple instantly. He was dark skinned and from a small country town in Natalia, Texas. When we first met, he talked a lot about his father and how he had suffered a stroke due to high blood pressure and diabetes. His admiration for his father was unique. I had never heard any man speak so highly about his dad. He spoke similarly of his grandfather on his mother's side, and how he'd always wanted to be like him. The stories he told me about his family were interesting and I began to get more and more involved with him.

Emilio attended church regularly with his mother and I thought that was sweet. He wanted to be a preacher because it was what his mother wanted. Emilio spoke well and was articulate, unlike me. I was not illiterate and didn't use Ebonics, I just spoke like I wasn't trying to be someone I wasn't. In other words, I didn't care how people viewed me. I spoke the way I spoke, and other people could take it or leave it. Emilio was cool with who I was. He never questioned my identity. He did ask what color my hair was, which I thought was very odd, but he was curious because he had never seen my natural hair color on a Black person. I didn't know what color my hair was and didn't pay it that much attention.

But when I met Emilio's brother Jessie about a month before their mother, he warned her that I was a "light, bright, and damn near white" Black girl.

Emilio's grandmother was from Mexico and she looked Mexican even though her father was Black. Her mother was Mexican. His grandmother spoke fluent Spanish and so did Emilio's entire family except him. He had the Spanish name but didn't speak a lick of Spanish. I always teased him about being a Black man with a Spanish name and how his last name should be "Perez" instead of Brooks. He hated his name and that was the reason he used Nino when introducing himself. Nino was a nickname that his sister Sandra called him.

When I met Emilio's mother, she instantly noticed my freckles. I've always hated my freckles because of kids calling me freckle face or pointing them out. It was another issue I had along with people asking about my ethnicity. His mother didn't know my hang-ups, so her comment was innocent. I did let Emilio know later that it was one of my pet peeves. And it was a big one. To me, it was like fingernails on a chalkboard. But his mother would also call me "fair skinned" a term used by many Black people of her generation. After meeting his entire family, there weren't any more conversations about skin complexion. Emilio didn't have a preference; he sought a good woman and mother for his future children. He had no children at the age of thirty and that made him a hot commodity to me. I sought a man that would give my son all the attention he needed, and Emilio was the perfect man to do so.

He took care of Myson, and in doing so, lifted a huge burden from my shoulders. Especially the day he offered to take care of Myson on the weekends while I worked. He was off on weekends so he would often drive from Natalia to San Antonio to pick up my son.

On the weekends, Myson would stay with my long-time friend, Tuter, but he often voiced his disdain for staying with her to Emilio. Myson was a mama's boy, and one morning as soon as I turned the corner after dropping him off at Tuter's house, he ran out the door and all the way down Hackberry and Grayson Streets to get to my job. He kept running no matter how much Tuter ran after him. He was seven years old and he wasn't stopping. She got into her car and had to persuade him to get in so she could take him to my job. He got into the car, but she'd lied and took him back to her house. Soon after that incident I met Emilio. Myson had just turned eight and I was only two weeks away from turning thirty-one. Emilio was weeks away from turning thirty-one. We were born thirty-four days apart.

He was a kind and gentle man and I could share anything with him knowing he wouldn't throw it in my face later. He wasn't that type of man. He didn't bring up my secrets and shortcomings whenever we argued like Bobby. I was comfortable around him. He never made me feel insecure. We went on many outings as a family, and never without Myson. He was dependable, reliable, and whenever he said he was coming to my apartment, he was there. He traveled over an hour daily to visit Myson and me.

During this time with Emilio, I was distracted from what was going on with my other friends. My friend Tiffany had gotten sick and her husband called to let me know that she was in the hospital.

I had taken her out for her birthday the day before, so I thought to myself, "Oh no, was it the food at Hometown Buffet?" It wasn't food poisoning. My dear friend had heard about Emilio, though they hadn't met. I was planning on introducing them soon, but she went into a coma and never came out of it.

Unfortunately, Tiffany lost her life due to a stroke. She had just turned twenty-six years old. Emilio had met Tiffany's husband John because he invited Myson to her children's birthday party and I also kept her kids when John needed a break. I didn't get to tell her about what was growing inside of me and she would never know how much I needed and appreciated her.

We met in Freshman Composition 1302 at San Antonio College in 1999. She was really good at English and history, but horrible at math. I would help her with math and she would edit my English papers. She made a difference in my life because of her style. She wasn't stuck-up and never acted privileged. She had a daughter by a Black man and a son with her husband. She was down to earth and often babysat Myson while I worked. She smoked and was a little overweight, but nothing drastic enough to cause a stroke. She had begun taking birth control pills a few months before the stroke, but I never knew of any underlying medical conditions. After her stroke I became pregnant with my daughter, Tahirah. John had moved on to another woman and she was pregnant at the same time as me. I was frustrated at John because Tiffany hadn't even been dead a year before he remarried and had another child. He moved on so fast it was like she never existed. I lost contact with John but we reconnected when he unknowingly moved into the same neighborhood where Emilio and I bought our first home.

My daughter and his daughter went to the same school and were both on the honor roll and did cheerleading.

John had a secret sexual appetite—he loved swinging. He and Tiffany had participated as swingers. It was *his* idea, not hers, but she went along with it out of her love for John. She wanted to make her husband happy, but it made her very depressed.

John had talked Tiffany into having sex with a Black guy while he watched. The guy was married, and he was in the military. Once she'd had sex with the Black guy, she began to really enjoy it, and she began taking birth control pills to prevent pregnancy. But there was a catch to John's sexual escapades. Since Tiffany had obliged his request to have sex with a Black man, it was his turn to have sex with a Black woman. Tiffany didn't straight up ask me to be a participant in this enigmatic lifestyle because she knew me and knew not to include me in their unorthodox marriage. However, we sat one Thanksgiving evening in the trailer home they had just purchased, and she drank and cried about how John was at a hotel room fucking another woman. A *Black* woman. I felt bad for her because she depended on John since she didn't work.

She was attending school to become a teacher and she had another two years before she'd complete her degree. I asked her why she wanted to become a teacher and she said to help kids. She was aware of the pay, but it was her passion to become a teacher and follow in her father's footsteps. He was a professor who taught English. Tiffany spoke highly of her dad, who had passed away when she was a teenager. That was before she got pregnant with her daughter.

Tiffany had her whole life ahead of her, but unfortunately it was cut short. She never had the opportunity to finish her degree and raise her two kids. I planned to introduce her to Smuvblkslk, and she was looking forward to meeting the man I talked her ears off about. Emilio and I had only been dating for two weeks before Tiffany had her stroke. She passed away a year later in 2001, but she left me in good hands, and if she was here today she would approve of Smuvblkslk.

Chapter Twenty-Nine

Angel Cakes

Emilio made my life less complicated. He brought so much joy and comfort into MySon's and my life when we needed it most. He was a caring and sensible man. My past hardships and the environment I was reared in didn't concern him. He accepted all of my demons head on, though there was a lot to drive anyone away. He sat for hours listening to me talk and cry about my mother. I always poured out my soul to him. There was nothing he didn't know about me before I became pregnant with his daughter. I was open and honest about it all and I expected the same from him. He was a man that I could finally depend on. Someone I could have a family and build with, and not risk it being destroyed. We had similar aspirations, so when we planned to have a child, we thought we were prepared. Until it happened. There is a saying: "Everybody thinks they are the greatest fighter until they get punched in the mouth." This is how my pregnancy went. We were well prepared until we weren't. But our daughter Tahirah being born completed our family of four. She was a beautiful baby and had a dimple on the right side of her cheek.

As an infant, Tahirah was unlike MySon's. Most of the time she slept throughout the night. If she did wake, Emilio and I would divide our time to get up and take care of her needs. We had twelve a.m. to four a.m. as the first shift and four a.m. to eight a.m. as the second shift. Each week, we would rotate between the first and second shifts. This worked best for us.

Tahirah began walking early in life. I don't ever remember her crawling, but at nine months old she took her first full steps. I was in Natalia and her grandmother told me that she wanted me to see something and placed Tahirah on the ground. Her dad was kneeling a few feet away with his arms held out and she walked to him. I was so excited and proud. Her grandmother got to see her first steps. But she was always advanced in everything that she did. One day when she was around eight months old she had pooped in her diaper. As I often did, I got directly in her face, inches away, and asked in my slow squeaky voice, "Did you poo poo?" I would blow my breath in her face as I spoke and she would blink her eyes. On this particular day, she beat me to it as I began to ask and she finished my question for me. I laughed so hard. My Angel Cakes talked! I had so many nicknames for her when she was young.

Tahirah learned to read when she was three years old. I taught her the alphabet and sounds early because I wanted her to be able to read and write when she began kindergarten. When raising Myson I learned that it was required, and if your child wasn't reading by kindergarten, they were behind. Tahirah was so advanced that when she began the Head Start program at three years old and the teachers were going over the alphabet and sounds, they had to ask her not to blurt out the answers to give the other students a chance to respond. I bought her all the learning games for Christmas. It was all educational. I look back at some of our home videos and watch with sadness because it seems like she couldn't be a child and play without me asking her about alphabet sounds and numbers. Emilio had to stop me and buy her regular toys as well. He thought I put too much stress on her to learn at a young age. But there was pressure from society and I didn't want her to be left behind. I was preparing her for the real

129

world. I wanted her to be the best. I did the same to MySon, but he would take the learning toys and put them in the closet. Years later I took them out and gave them to Tahirah.

Tahirah turned one year old a few months before I graduated from the University of Texas. Emilio had wanted to get married before Tahirah was born, but I wasn't ready. It wasn't until a week before graduation that we decided to wed. I regretted not marrying Emilio sooner, but my first marriage had been a nightmare and I didn't want another divorce if it didn't work out. We got married and made our family official. We had bigger plans for our life together, so we began our journey as husband and wife.

Chapter Thirty

Home Sweet Home

I was a wife and a mother of *two* kids. It's funny, I think back on how I said that I would *never* remarry or have any more kids. Prior to meeting Emilio, Myson and I planned to leave San Antonio and move to Atlanta, Georgia. I felt there was better opportunity there for a Black woman to achieve success than in San Antonio. But things changed after I met Emilio and the move to Atlanta was put on hold. He didn't want to leave his family. I didn't want to leave my family either, but it would have given me more opportunities in a business technology career. The move to Atlanta didn't happen; instead, we discussed buying a home in San Antonio. Our kids needed a backyard to play in and Myson really wanted a dog. He was ten years old and he had been asking for a dog for years.

Emilio and I began looking for pre-existing homes but we couldn't find anything of interest, so Emilio suggested we build, and explained that it was not expensive to build a brand new home. We began researching further, looking at new subdivisions, and he was right about it being better to build a new home. We were living in the Alamo Heights area at the time, after I had moved from the northeast side of town. I was familiar with the area, but I wanted to have that country-but-city environment, so we chose an area that didn't have a bus line within two miles and no other subdivisions nearby. It was close to the highway, and at the time wasn't too far from Emilio's and my jobs.

In February 2006 we signed the contract to have the 2,652 square foot home built on Rothberger Way, and within five months we were homeowners. I remember the day we closed on the house we bought Church's Chicken and sat on the kitchen floor eating because we hadn't moved in yet. We parked the car in the garage and turned on some music. We were so excited because the place was huge and the kids could have their own bedrooms and a backyard. We began moving in the next day.

Life was good in the neighborhood. There were very few homes built and we began to get acquainted with our new neighbors who had moved in a few months before us.

They were all married couples with kids. The only problem was the kids that were the same age as my kids were opposite genders, so my kids didn't have any neighbors close by to play with. Myson was fourteen when we moved into the home, so he met friends from school and would play with them. They didn't live in our neighborhood but were close by. Tahirah was four years old. My kids grew fast, before my very eyes, and I began wondering about the other half of me. I saw the love and interaction between Emilio and the kids and couldn't help but feel sorrow. I missed my daddy. I missed my mom. I knew they were looking down on me and very proud of the accomplishments and progress I had made in life. I was the rose Tupac talked about that grew from the concrete. I had escaped the ghetto and now my kids were being raised in a *home*. They would never know what it was like to miss a meal or be surrounded by gunshots and violence. I was going to work until I couldn't work anymore to provide for them and give them a much better life than I had at their age. We got a Shih Tzu dog and named him BobbyTee. It was my idea to put my children's names into the name of the dog. I had accomplished what I set out to do with my husband by my side. We made Rothberger Way our home.

Chapter Thirty-One

DNA

*I*t was December 2009 and I was sitting at my desk preparing to leave work for the extended Christmas break when I decided to Google his name one last time before I gave up my search for good. I had been searching off and on for about twelve years. Google was my friend on this day. I Googled DeWhight's name and there was a listing from the white pages: *DeWhight Wilson in Littleton, Colorado.*

It had a telephone number *and* an address. I held onto the address for a few days and then I spoke with Emilio about writing him. I didn't want to call, so I sent a handwritten letter to the address in search of my biological father. I felt in my heart that this was the correct DeWhight because of the unique way he spelled his name. When I searched for his name, I always spelled it Dwhight or Dwight but never DeWhight. I was ready for my search to end. I wanted to confront the root of my daddy issues and DeWhight was the key.

I was officially on Christmas break when I sat at the kitchen table and wrote the letter by hand. I didn't know how to address it and I kept crumbling up pieces of notebook papers and shooting baskets because of mistakes with my penmanship and grammar. I wrote about my mother and the information that she passed along about him. I asked if he had frequented the Pig Stand on Broadway in San Antonio, Texas. If he was born in Denver, Colorado and stationed in the military. I completed the letter and mailed it the next day.

I didn't know if I would receive a response. I was anxious and nervous, but my heart told me that my search was over and I had found the real DeWhight.

On December 26, 2009, Myson and I were at South Park Mall doing some after-Christmas shopping. We were at the ice cream shop when my cell phone rang. The display showed a number calling from Colorado. My heart went racing and I told Myson it might be DeWhight because it was someone calling from Colorado. I moved out of the line and asked Myson to get my ice cream while I answered my phone. It was DeWhight! I asked him about everything my mother told me, and he confirmed it. He kept saying, "I'm trying to wrap my brain around all of this."

He said he was basically "wild" when he was young, and he'd had many women. I don't know if he even remembered my mother because it was so long ago.

There was so much background noise from the mall I asked him to call me the next day. I was so excited and couldn't wait to talk more with him. One of the things I asked on the phone was if he was a light-skinned Black because I wanted to know my ethnicity and where I got my light skin. He said he wasn't Black; he was an Indian. I was thinking to myself, *an Indian? How is my hair kinky and you're an Indian?* But I didn't ask any more questions as we hung up. I told Myson about the conversation and went home to tell my husband as well. I waited for DeWhight to phone the next day and he called like he said he would. It was close to twelve noon when he called. We talked a little more and I told him that my mother was no longer living and that she had committed suicide. I asked if he wanted me to send pictures to help jog his memory and he agreed. But I was getting frustrated because he kept saying, "Tammy, I don't know what to tell you." He said my name just like my grandmother and his voice sounded aged and raspy. I can still hear it. It sounded as though he smoked cigarettes his entire life. I told him that I had two kids. He asked what color they were and whether they were light skinned. I thought it was an *odd* question, but I told him they were both light skinned. My picture of him became distorted like a bad connection. It wasn't what I had envisioned. We spoke briefly and I confirmed that I would be sending him photos. I'm a well-organized person and didn't procrastinate. I gathered pictures immediately of my mother, my family, and me, and sent them the following day. I calculated the time it would take for him to receive them. I told my kids that hopefully they would get to know their grandfather, and if he needed anything I would accommodate him since he was older. I didn't know if he had family, was married, or had other children. He didn't say and I didn't ask. I wanted to know if I had his DNA, and based on my conversation with him, it appeared that I did.

DeWhight seemed strategic in his correspondence with me. He'd called me the day after Christmas in 2009, and I received his letter after the New Year. He didn't call but sent a typed letter explaining that he could no longer help me with my search for my biological father, and that he wished me good luck. He included the pictures I had sent him inside the envelope. After reading the letter I wanted to cry or throw-up, maybe both. But I didn't do either.

What the hell did he mean he could no longer help me with my search? *Was* he my father? He confirmed everything my mother told me, but as soon as I sent him pictures, he wished me luck with my search? I was crushed. I showed the letter to my husband and told my kids what happened. I went into a depression and ruined everyone's holiday fun because I wanted to stay locked in my room and not come out. This is what I did for almost a week. My kids and hubby sympathized with me. I came out of my depression when Myson came to me and said, "Mama, you don't need him. You got us who love you. You don't need him."

My husband continued with, "It's his loss because you are an amazing woman." My daughter agreed with Myson and my husband, and her gentle hug brought out the tears I held inside. The love and reassurance I got from them was all I needed. I began to pull myself together after that. But I thought about DeWhight's words and wondered why he sent a typed letter instead of a handwritten one. It seemed like it was from an attorney's office instead of personally from him. He didn't confirm or deny that he was my father, but not acknowledging, that hurt. It was as if I didn't exist. *I do exist. I'm here, motherfucker and it wasn't my choice!* I was angry, bitter, and confused. I was better off not even reaching out to him. He had left me even more devastated than I already was about my ethnicity. Why had he confirmed everything my mother said over the phone, then change his tune after he received my pictures? My husband said it must've been because of him; he didn't like his dark skin. I said if he didn't like dark skin he could go fuck himself. What the hell, Indian? Indian? I kept replaying his words in my head. Him asking if my kids were light skinned. Did it matter? Apparently to him it did. I saw his number on my home phone Caller ID once. I didn't return his call and told myself he would call back if it was important, but he never did. I was ready to turn the page and move on. I wasn't going to beg anyone to acknowledge me. I pondered that he might be married with a family and didn't want anyone to know about his past transgressions. He would rob me of knowing who I was, and it was fine with him, even though it was cruel to me. I wanted to at least see a picture of the man who gave me life, but then again, he sent a typed letter and that showed me that I wasn't even worthy of his penmanship.

I was so confused that I continued to search for him hoping he wasn't the one, and my real father would be more accepting of me. I read online about other people looking for their biological family and I shared my story. One responder told me to take the envelope that he sent and have it swabbed for his saliva. Maybe he licked it and they could get his DNA from it. I'd never thought of that, and I was desperate, so I conversed with my husband and he said to do whatever it took for me to get closure.

I searched online for DNA testing laboratories and chose the one I thought was the best according to research and reviews. I took the envelope to a DNA laboratory not too far from where I lived. I explained to the technician what I was trying to achieve. She told me that the standard method of extracting saliva from an envelope had a lower success ratio than other methods. If I could do a more expensive test, there was a greater chance of extracting the DNA, but that was double the price. I asked if it was possible to try the less expensive method first, and if it didn't yield enough DNA, try the more expensive method. She explained that I could only choose one because the envelope wouldn't have enough DNA to try both. I wanted to know if DeWhight was my father, so I agreed to try the more expensive method and pay double the price for the test. It was $500.

My results were ready within two weeks. I prayed that the envelope with his saliva contained enough DNA to bring closure to my biological father's mystery. I opened the results and was expecting to see results like on the Maury Povich TV show: "DeWhight is 99.9% the biological father of Tammy." Instead, I sank further into despair, and my bank account deduction of $500 was worthless. The envelope didn't yield enough DNA so my results were inconclusive. They couldn't confirm or deny paternity from the small sample size extracted from the envelope. I was exhausted, but I continued to search. I had unanswered questions about me.

Years had passed since I'd heard from DeWhight. I still had his phone number saved in my contacts list, but I wasn't calling him. I had moved on. Well, I thought I had moved on until I read about two companies called, 23andMe and AncestryDNA. These companies could send a DNA test kit in the mail. You'd do a swab test, then send the kit back to them, and they could match your DNA to relatives that had done the same. I was interested the more I read about it. I figured if DeWhight didn't want anything to do with me then I could at least build a connection or relationship with other family members. I spoke to my husband again and he said that I should take the test. I asked him to take the test too so he could find out his history, and then our daughter would know her history from both sides. He wasn't seeking any biological parents like me, but he agreed to take the test, and so did his mother. Our results came back within six weeks and the test confirmed my husband and his mother were mother and son. This wasn't a surprise. Emilio's results showed that he was over 25% Native American. His lineage is from Mexico. His mother showed over 25% Native American too. Her mother was from Mexico and was biracial. DeWhight's claims of being Indian and the test didn't make sense. My results showed I was only 3% Native American. My mother's grandmother was Cherokee Indian, so I figured the amount came from my great-grandmother on my maternal side. I looked for DNA matches and found a second cousin from DeWhight's side of the family. I tried contacting her to get more information, but she never responded. I was out $99 dollars and still had no closure. I joined the 23andMe forum and learned that people saw better results with AncestryDNA if they were seeking relatives. They had a larger database and could help connect with more relatives.

In June 2017, I took the AncestryDNA test, and I received my DNA results back on July 02, 2017. I looked at my results and saw close relatives under my matches. It was Dorothy and Deleon, some first cousins. Dorothy and Deleon were DeWhight's siblings. Their DNA results were managed by Dorothy's husband. I began messaging anyone that was related to branches that lead to DeWhight Wilson's family tree. I met one lady named Monica. I call her my cousin because she was very familiar with Dorothy's husband and she had spoken to Dorothy in the past. She gave me Dorothy's contact information because she saw that my DNA was matched to hers.

On July 04, 2017 I wrote and sent Dorothy pictures of me and told her I was her niece and DeWhight was my father. She never responded. I sent a message to her husband through AncestryDNA letting him know that I wrote her and to make sure she received my email but he didn't respond. This seemed odd, how they ignored me. I continued to correspond with Monica through messages and text. She couldn't understand their silence either. She decided to email Dorothy's husband to see how he was and to get the message through that I was trying to reach his wife. He sent Monica an email saying DeWhight had passed away and that it was too soon for his wife to have to deal with me. She thought they would reach out to me soon but they were in mourning at the time. I could understand, so I waited, but got nothing from Dorothy's husband.

DeWhight was deceased and I didn't feel any sadness. I felt angry. He was the man I spoke to in 2009, who I sent pictures to, and he'd sent me a letter saying he couldn't help me with my search. It *was* him like I thought! That was my sperm donor! I felt more rejected than I had before. I wanted to find out how he died and if he had any medical conditions that my children and I needed to be aware of. That selfish son of a bitch robbed me of my history and his living siblings were doing the same. What kind of soulless human beings were they?

I could see pictures of DeWhight's family from Monica's tree. She gave me full access to her tree and sent all pictures of his family, but she didn't have any pictures of DeWhight. I had pictures of my paternal grandmother, and her census records showed that she was "Indian." My paternal grandfather's census records also read "Indian." DeWhight was correct. *He was Indian.* But my paternal grandmother was dark skinned and she didn't look anything like an Indian that you'd see on TV. She was Black according to today's society. I wanted to see a picture of my grandfather, but they didn't have any. I wanted to see where I got my light skin. I researched further and found my grandfather's mother, and she looked Irish. Their surname is Alnutt. She was the lightest of her family. Her mother, father, and siblings were all dark skinned. I examined the family picture that was taken and none of her siblings or mother and father smiled. The picture looked eerie. Mysterious. I didn't know what to think.

On November 15, 2017, I received a message from a family member on DeWhight's side asking questions about my Campbell family, trying to see how we were related. It was my first cousin's husband, Tony. I explained to him that his wife was related to me on my paternal side (DeWhightDwight), not my maternal side. I told him that my estranged biological father was DeWhight. He was shocked because he knew DeWhight and never heard that he had children. He called him by the nickname, Puddie. He told me that DeWhight passed away in 2016 from a kidney disease, PKD (Poly-Cystic

Kidney Disease). He gave me a little history about how DeWhight retired from the military, and that when he returned home he lived with his sister. He and his brothers opened a painting business, and then DeWhight opened his own business. He married twice. He sent me pictures of DeWhight and his second wife. I *finally* received pictures of the family. I was elated and thanked him. I sent him pictures of me and my children. He said that he would see if he could find more pictures of DeWhight and that he would contact Dorothy. He must have contacted Dorothy soon after because I never heard from him again.

Chapter Thirty-Two

Closure

I'm sitting here in my newly-built home that Emilio and I purchased a few months ago. We sold our Rothberger Way home and we have settled into our final residence in life. Emilio and I have been together for almost two decades. We have been through so much, but we have continued to stay strong. One thing I learned throughout our relationship was that he too suffers from his own daddy issues, though he chooses to cope with his by staying in denial. But as I examine his family story, his father had his own daddy issues too. It seems like many people suffer the same issues and it becomes a never-ending cycle.

I'm sure Myson has daddy issues too, even though he says he doesn't because he was raised with a daddy, Emilio. Myson has moved to Missouri to further his career because he felt that San Antonio wasn't the place for a Black man to become successful. No matter where Myson is, he and his sister sit on an imaginary swing together inside of my heart. He and Tahirah will always be my Sonshine and my Angel Cakes.

Tahirah graduated high school in 2020, the year the Covid-19 pandemic swept through the world. She graduated from her prestigious high school *cum laude* and has earned her associate degree while in high school. She is in the process of choosing a four-year institution to complete her doctorate in pharmacy.

Emilio and I are taking it day by day with the uncertainties in life. I'm waiting for the next cousin to match my DNA and learn about their stories of identity crisis.

On AncestryDNA I was notified of many cousins on DeWhight's side of the family. I had a cousin Troy who was in the same situation as me, looking for answers about who his biological father was. When Troy's results came back, he was matched as parent and child with DeWhight's brother, Deleon, who had taken the AncestryDNA test. Dorothy's husband immediately hid the results and they were no longer available on the website. Dorothy and Deleon's DNA results were also no longer available. But I have screenshots of the DNA matches and that's good enough for me.

Troy and I formed a bond and we talk or text with each other often. We met another first cousin, Craig, who was very close to DeWhight and his brothers. He knew them well. He was able to give Troy and I much-needed history about the Wilson family. He told us that our grandparents were cousins, and the reason a lot of our DNA was slightly off on AncestryDNA is because of that mixing of the same blood. Troy and I share more segments of DNA than Craig and I do, even though his father and DeWhight were brothers. Craig's results showed him and me as first or second cousins.

On the Wilson side of the family there were a lot of cousins married to each other. I found this very strange because none of this was prevalent on my maternal side. I remember Craig telling Troy and me, "You know, our grandparents being cousins, it is what it is, and ain't nothing we can do about it. Now you know, and no one can throw it in your face."

I often wondered how it affected our biological makeup if people with the same DNA had children together. How were their organs affected? What type of genetic deficiencies were handed down from generation to generation?

The kidney disease DeWhight died from was rampant in the Wilson family medical ailments. I tested negative for PKD after I was advised by Tony to get tested. His wife tested negative too.

Although I never heard from Tony again after Dorothy was notified about my desire for family history, he provided so much insight by sending me pictures of DeWhight, and giving me the backstory of how he and his brothers had a painting company and he branched off to own his own business. I don't need to wonder how DeWhight looked anymore. I know how he looked. I know where the *light skin* originated. I know the Indian heritage. I finally got what I had been searching for, for over twenty years.

I have a face.

I have his history.

I have an identity.

I have my closure.

I can finally bury my daddy issues and start the healing process.

Tahirah(17)   Myson(27)

Tammy & Myson

Tahirah(5)

Emilio(31)

Tina(54)   Terrie(47)   Tammy(50)

Terrie   Richard   Debbie   Edward

Bobbie Jean and Pee Tee's Children

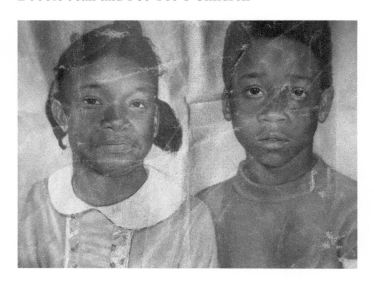

Tina(8)   Edward(6)

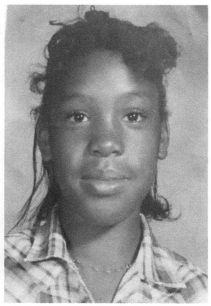

Tammy(9)   Terrie(9)

Argentina Campbell Smith   Carl Edward Campbell

Carla Marie Campbell   Meoisha Nicole Campbell

Barbara Jean Cline(Campbell) - mother

James Edward Campbell Sr.- father

Emma Jane Hughes (Cline)- maternal grandmother

Emma   Tom Cline (T.C)- maternal grandfather

Sammie Lee Maney (Hughes)- maternal great-great grandmother

Dora Ross Baily- maternal great, great, great grandmother

Dewhight Wilson

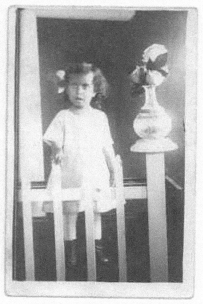

Alice Mercer Wilson – paternal grandmother

Delores Jean Wilson (paternal aunt)

Ancestry Census Records

Source Citation for U.S., Indian Census Rolls, 1885-1940

×

U.S., Indian Census Rolls, 1885-1940

⊶⊲ Ancestry Record

🛈 Citation Details

🔗 Associated Facts

📷 Media

View Image

View Record

Name	Delores Jean Wilson
Date of Birth	1935
Age	5
Gender	Female
Marital Status	Single
Relation to Head of Household	Daughter
Tribe	Pottawatomie
Reservation	Potawatomi
Agency	Potawatomi
State	Kansas
Last Census Number	1067
Previous Census Number	991
Census Date	1 Jan 1940
Neighbors	View others on page
Household Members	

Close

🗑 REMOVE

159

1930 United States Federal Census

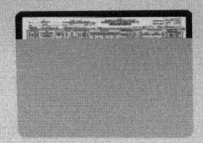

VIEW IMAGE

VIEW RECORD

Name	Leroy Wilson
Birth Year	abt 1906
Gender	Male
Race	Indian
Age in 1930	24
Birthplace	Missouri
Marital Status	Married
Relation to Head of House	Boarder
Home in 1930	Chicago, Cook, Illinois, USA
Map of Home	Chicago, Cook, Illinois
Street Address	Waller

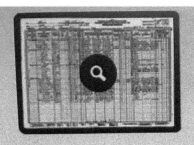

Name	**Alice Wilson**
Birth Year	**abt 1911**
Gender	**Female**
Race	**Indian**
Age in 1930	**19**
Birthplace	**Missouri**
Marital Status	**Married**
Relation to Head of House	**Boarder**
Home in 1930	**Chicago, Cook, Illinois, USA**
Map of Home	**Chicago, Cook, Illinois**
Street Address	**Waller**

James Nelson Alnutt family

Top (Lottie, Will, Pearl, Kate, Frank)

Bottom(Carrie Alnutt Wilson-paternal great grandmother)

James Nelson(paternal great, great grandfather),

Adline Nelson (Edwards)-paternal great, great grandmother)

 Bessie

Thank you for reading *Daddy Issues*. I hope you enjoyed it.

9 781732 276864